MENtally

Challenged

Dedicated to Men

If you don't know, now you know.

PART I

New Year New Friends

Here we are and the year is over already. It's New Year's
Eve so my girlfriend and I are ready to bring it in right.
Last year was a rough year for me but my girl Desire was
even more anxious to leave it behind. I had a horrible
job and by that I mean, hostile environment. Working a
low grade position for a meaningless corporation that
would like to think they own you, but I've been hanging
in there three years now. Three years of lies, no
employee morale, stealing, and racism. That's how me
and my best friend met. She was working with this
belligerent bold ass "I think I'm God" prick that uses our

own people against us to avoid any discrimination lawsuits. We sat down and began talking one day, just venting about the crazy place and noticed we had a lot in common. At the same time we were from two different sides of the track but got along great. We ended up sharing our stories and decided to hang out sometime. I loved going out clubbing and kicking it at the bars but I wasn't too sure Miss. Sophisticated could roll with my kind of party.

I always offered but I couldn't get that girl out if I paid her. She wasn't having it! She says "I'm not about to do my hair, put on a sexy dress, some high ass heels, to go out and dance my ass off for some man to stand behind me and think he's getting some at the end of the night! I don't think so. I'll stay at home and drink my Lime-a-Rita!" I couldn't blame her because that's all I did when I went out anyways so she wasn't missing out on anything.

Our friendship really hit it off over the next few months and within a blink the New Year was approaching. She came by my desk at work and asked if I wanted to go to this New Year's Eve party. I had never been to one and was definitely down to ride, until she told me the tickets were a little expensive. I said "Well, who all is going to be at this party the reason I have to spend so much money?" Now I was single, in my 40s, no kids, never married, and was very ready for a committed relationship. She says "We should go. I heard there will be some eligible bachelors there so we need to check it out. Not for me, but at least for you." Sister girl had more hope than I did. I've been around long enough and hadn't found Mr. Right yet. She proceeded to tell me it was formal attire, free champagne, food, and two floors of ballroom fun. Old school was on the top floor and new school was on the bottom. That's all she needed to say.

I knew I had to work, as usual. Just like that job to give you the most fucked up schedule they can, constantly screwing you! I must say I was looking for new employment to come in the New Year myself. You see, Desire didn't take any shit! She's not a woman to let a job believe she needs them so they can abuse her. Once you start messing around with her, your clock is ticking. She'll be gone and you won't even see it coming. She was too smart to be there anyway. I hoped she would find a better job in the New Year as well.

A week before the dance we decided to try on our dresses. I had one in my closet perfect for the event. She brought hers over and it was gorgeous. She said she bought it years ago for her reception, at the time she was engaged but they never married and eventually broke up. Her dress however, was stunning and nobody at that party would be able to compete. I woke up the morning of December 31st and it was snowing so much I could barely get out of the parking lot. I figured it would stop eventually, later on in the day. I usually work mid shift anyways so by night fall I should be good. Boy was I wrong about that one, by nine o'clock that night it was a blizzard outside. Fortunately, the party was closer to me than home was.

She called and said she was on her way there but she had to go back because she forgot the tickets. Finally, she made it right before I got off work. Her and this guy she'd been talking to for a while were kind of remaining friends and she was very surprised he drove her around in all that snow knowing how much he likes to drink. It was New Year's Eve; all people do that day is drink. Still, she didn't realize he cared that much. They had good times but weren't a good fit for each other. He knew she deserved better and was willing to let her go to find it.

In the meantime, I got off of work and met her in the hotel lobby. I saw so many people and noticed a lot of men walking around without women on their arms so I ran into the bathroom and changed faster than you could say boo. I made sure I brought my A game, ready and waiting to find me an attractive business man.

Desire had no expectations about what the night would bring. All she wanted to do was be the best dressed. She pissed all the women off strutting around in this gorgeous gold silk gown that clearly wasn't going to be duplicated. Hers was one of a kind.

I got to give her props because my friend shut it down like only her classy ass can. We walked around from one level to the next, enjoying the atmosphere and fruity drinks. The music upstairs was moving me for a minute so we got on the dance floor and kicked it for a little while. Desire was young but she had an old soul. She loved 90s music and good food. Honey, the girl can eat! She can put it away like nobody can. But I'm still trying to figure out where it goes. She's light skinned, long dark hair, full lips, and brown eyes, stands about 5'4", and has a body in perfect proportion. God did not bless her with too much of one thing; he gave her a little bit of everything. She was a wonderful woman and I had hopes that she'd meet a wonderful man to make a believer out of both of us.

See one thing we had in common was men. We both had our share of cheating, lying, and abusive sorry ass men! Girlfriend took her experiences a little different than me. She tried her best to be successful at things that worked for her, like money. She felt like love was one thing that never has and never will work for her. I could tell in my months of getting to know her she was becoming more comfortable and accepting of the single life. It was an adjustment coming from a long term relationship and failed dates after. She just wanted a break from the joke we call love.

Me on the other hand, I've been single for years and was very well used to it but that did not mean I wanted to be. I came to this party open minded, hoping to meet someone to spend time with. All I ended up with was a stalking over weight Rick Ross look alike that would not leave me alone. What else is new? I think I'm going to start dating some men in a different race because black men got me twisted.

Mr. Busted was going to get the point though because Desire didn't play that. She was very protective and watched all of her surroundings. He started standing in dark corners and popping up behind me on the dance floor so I warned him that was going to get him hurt. We had each other's back so no man was going to be trying nothing he didn't have no business trying. The party calmed down as we waited for the midnight hour to arrive so we decided to take a stroll downstairs to take some pictures.

I sat and posed as she snapped me sitting in the chair with my Happy New Year crown on. As I started taking pictures of her though I could tell she wasn't too much up for smiling but was happy to show off her dress. Out of nowhere two gentlemen just jumped in her picture as I was taking it. Her face was hilarious as it totally read "No they didn't!" They introduced themselves and you could tell one was really feeling Desire. He couldn't take his eyes off of her so I figured the picture thing was a way of running interference. For a second she cracked a smile when Chicago asked if she was with anyone and said he'd look for her later to dance. She said okay and went on like nothing ever happened. See me, I wouldn't have let that conversation end that quickly but she wasn't really optimistic on meeting someone that night anyways. Here, I'll let her tell you how it all went down.

The Amazing 90

"Better 90 days than six months or a year later." There it was, the bomb I had been expecting and suppressing. Chicago was now the very thing I'd been trying to avoid. Here I was young, fine, and very happy with the new love I'd found in my new year. BOOM! He's somewhat pulling back and says I'm moving forward. We had shared 90 days of wonderful. Communication was constant, the chemistry was off the chain, and everything was falling into place. When we met, New Year's Eve, I was at a party looking my best and was

*approached by a handsome gentleman that asked me to
dance. With optimism I said yes, and as soon as we took
the floor he placed his arms around me and his grip was
definitely not going to let me go. Thank God because I
know I can't slow dance!*

*The night brought us further into conversation and we
seemed to share a connection. I decided to call it a
night, feeling not really interested. Remembering that
this is how it always begins, love, something that life has
shown does not work for me. We exchanged numbers
anyway and I told him I was going to find my girlfriend.
He said to find him before I left and boy did he mean it. I
left and didn't find him but that definitely didn't stop
him from pursuing me through text. Persistently, he
asked to see me several times before he went back to
Chicago, but in that storm I definitely wasn't getting out.*

*In days our text became more frequent. In weeks our
text became routine good mornings, miss yous, and
goodnights. The intellectual intimacy was the deepest*

I'd ever had and we were really growing closer as friends getting to know each other. Our conversations were limitless; we talked about everything there was to talk about. We had so much in common and at the same time could really teach each other some things. We both loved music, movies, and come to find out he even writes music. He's done a lot of traveling and I've done none so I enjoyed listening to him talk about the different places he's been and where he wanted to go. I love food on the other hand and I was really surprised that he was so open minded to trying some new things.

In a month all of that became "I can't wait to see you in two weeks." Of course before diving into this we talked about the distance. He's in Chicago and I was in Kansas City. He said we could meet up half way in STL like once a month though. In my mind, I was okay with it figuring if the relationship progressed we were just five or six hours apart. That's nothing to me, I can leave in the morning and be there that afternoon. We had a lot of potential so I was willing to come quite often if we got to that point but for now I was just seeing where things were going.

In no time I found myself in the windy city going to spend six days with someone I hadn't seen in a month and had only spent half an hour with. I was so nervous and so excited at the same time. I got off my flight and he had already text me, "That must be you that flew over me because my heart just skipped a beat." I figured he was nervous as hell too. As I walked out of baggage claim there he was. He gets out of the car and greets me with the sweetest embrace, a big hug and a pleasant kiss on the cheek. I couldn't stop thinking is this real, am I really doing this. Funny thought, no matter how disappointing love was previously we always give it a second time around. Or should I say 10th, 11th, and 12th! Porsha text's me asking "Girl is he crazy? Are you ok?" I told her I was alright, he was really nice, and that I'll send 911 if anything goes down! I wasn't worried at all with him though, he was cool.

We spent the first three days at the Hard Rock Hotel for Valentine's Day. Our first moment alone in a room and there was so much anticipation and silence, somewhat of an awkward feeling not knowing what to do or say. He definitely took the time to make me feel very special with flowers, strawberries, wine, and gifts. Everything was so natural I thought it had to be something special this time. The good thing you wait all your life for. I decided this was it, no holding back. You know, trying not to think they're all the same. No rules, games, private thoughts.... I wasn't going to let a broken heart and scars keep me from a wonderful man.

He took me out for dinner to a beautiful restaurant ninety five stories in the sky. Yes, I said ninety five....your ears even pop on the way up. The view was beautiful but his eyes were amazing. As he was talking I remember one moment where I took a second and watched him watching me. He was really excited too and I loved every minute of it. Oh, and dinner was delicious by the way...just not that important. We rode around downtown on the way back to the hotel; anyone who knows me knows I definitely ate enough for me and him. The magnificent mile was beautiful, this gorgeous strip of every store I love all on one street. Everything I thought it would be.

This was wonderful, something I was not exactly expecting. I'd never done long distance before but we clearly had what it takes to make it work. I was happy, he was happy, no problems. We communicated so well even I was confident if some were to come we would be able to talk through them. This wasn't like talking to someone you never met before, you see them and it's not the same. This definitely wasn't anything like a blind date either. The room was nice; no view necessary, all we saw was each other anyway. I was so nervous as we layed in bed looking at a movie that neither of us was really watching, just sitting there in our own thoughts. We talked about our backgrounds, and I told him thanks for dinner. I was actually having the greatest time I'd had in years and was very happy to be sharing it with him.

Now came the hard part. I got up, took a long shower and put on something sexy he said he'd never had before. Desire does not do lingerie but for him I didn't mind. I was so uncomfortable in it but I was wearing the hell out of it at the same time. I asked him was he ready and he seemed a little nervous too but was speechless when I appeared before him looking absolutely gorgeous. I must say I was pretty damn irresistible!

Let me tell you, the man had the best smelling massage oil with eucalyptus that relaxes you instantly. I layed there on my stomach, hair cascading down my back as he began to massage me from head to toe. I had to wonder does he just grip me like that or he grips everybody like that. As soon as my muscles relaxed he turned me over and wrapped his tongue around my toes, all thoughts ceased. He kissed me up my thighs and once his tongue was stroking my clict paralyzing my mind with every lick I knew I was gone, couldn't think or move. My body was throbbing, pulsating, and oozing juices like a sponge waiting for him to penetrate and feel my warm walls squeeze him tightly.

As his pipe reaches my ocean, parting my sea with every thrust my body was communicating every pleasure with him. I couldn't control my moans, my mind, nothing. He found my g-spot as he was working me every way but left. I felt his body begin to erupt and I exploded from the inside out. Smiling upon his face of satisfaction, I was ready to do it all over again.

The days grew sweeter and sweeter; we really enjoyed each other all the time. Publicly people could see how happy we were together and feel the vibes we were spinning off each other. Our chemistry was something we knew we'd never find again. I know he was thinking more than like and I was thinking the same too. The last three days we spent at his home. He had a nice place, surprised so clean for a man. Still as sweet as ever, had something waiting for me on the bed. He was always thoughtful, my favorite quality in a man. I met his brother and family while I was there, and was a little taken back by that but I went with it. I never got a feeling of ill intentions with him. No major issues and I say that because we all have some but he didn't even seem to care about the things you know men usually focus on like sex. I take that back, I'm sure he cared but at least he didn't act like it. We were just having a good time. That's what I loved the most.

I was overwhelmed with thoughts every moment I spent with him, even making love. He was really into pleasing me and of course I loved that. I've never been comfortable with any man sexually but I said if this was it, I'm all in. His arms stayed around me all the time. We went out to a jazz event and I made sure I looked my best. Straight up head turner dressed to shut it down! As usual, we smiled the entire night listening to the entertainment, rocking our fedoras, and stuck in every moment of laughter. You could tell I loved looking my *best for him. I'm a big believer in you represent your man at all times, and honey I was definitely representing! He had a grip on me from the night we met, things were really going great but I still had somewhat of a guard up. Ok, a really big guard!*

The days were going by so fast and before I knew it my flight was departing in three hours. Sadness came over me and I couldn't really tell how he felt until he came in his bedroom after putting my bags in the car, and hugged me like time was going to stand still just for us. I left him something special on his night stand, a good thank you for the vacation. And there I was, on my flight home, thinking of the amazing trip I just had with someone I could really feel. I began missing him immediately, attempting to hold it together by the time my plane landed. Couldn't even wait to let him know I made it safely, wondering if he felt the same as I did.

Inside I was jumping for joy and weeping the distance until I see him again. I had no excuses to be negative this time. He was genuine, sincere, respectful, responsible, and very protective. Being in two different cities, you can't say the usual all he wants is sex. If anything, I desired it more than him. Once I made it home, things really went to another level. We wanted to see each other the first time but we really wanted to see each other again after. Our constant text and routine calls increased and I didn't even think we could talk any more than we already did. We couldn't get enough of each other. This was kind of getting serious real quick and I could tell he was starting to think about the future.

Questions about marriage scenarios and relocation made that obvious. I was cool with it though, I had thought about some of it myself. If I moved there, if he moved here, or even if we just moved somewhere together. I was sticking with taking it slow though; I've had enough heartbreak for one life time and didn't need anymore. I was surprised I got that far. Don't get me wrong, I really like him and all but I had a wall up the size of Texas. He told me he tore his ACL one day and was having surgery soon, didn't sound like a big deal at the time. I knew his knee was messed up when I was there but wasn't aware it was that bad. I told him I would come take care of him if he wanted me to but he said he'd be alright. Little did I know that would change everything.

What The Hell!

Before I knew it the surgery date was here, he let me know when he was going in and called me when he got home. I was kind of worried since he sounded so bad but he slept it off and seemed alright. I sent him something sweet since my sweet ass couldn't be there and I checked on him constantly. We started plotting on the next trip but he said he wanted to wait until after the doctor appointments settled down.

I was at work when he sent me a picture of the bed with an "I miss you." All I thought was let me get my ass on up out this damn job and go check on my love. If he needed me I was on my way with no delays, but he said he was alright with me coming next month. A week later that changed, he said he needed me on my next weekend off, no questions asked I booked the tickets that night. I was now going to see him next week and couldn't wait I was so excited. Here I was all packed and ready to go. We'd been talking about how anxious we were to see each other again until I was off of work and on my way to the airport. I said "Baby I really can't wait to feel your arms around me." He said "These arms need to hold you." That was the last time I spoke to Chicago, I mean the Chicago I knew.

That plane couldn't move fast enough! How fast do they go, 200 or 300 miles an hour, something like that, whatever it was it wasn't good enough. I needed a jet to get to my love! To top it all off, I had a stopping flight with a layover. Finally, the plane landed and I had just enough time to change into my sexy heels, fix my hair, and call him. Next time I'll remember to just drive, it would've gone much faster. Sure enough he was pulling up in no time and there were the butterflies. He got out the car, knee brace and all. Not wanting him to lift a finger, I told him get back in and got my bags myself.

I was back where I'd longed to be for over a month, but wait a minute, something wasn't right. He was so distant, in every way possible. I felt it as soon as I got in the car. Every day there after he was someone else, surgery had really depressed him. I knew something was wrong because things weren't quite like they used to be and it didn't scare me or anything, I just wanted to make him happy. I figured I'll make him smile, that's what I'm here for. He said he needed me and here I am, ready to do whatever he desired. Hello, that is my name! Ice his knee, cook a good meal, rub his back, what's that song Jill Scott has….do you want it on your collard greens, candy sweets, and pinto beans! I was ready to put it DOWN!

Whatever he wanted, I was there to deliver. About to go straight up Anita Baker on his ass and give him the best that I got, OK! It wasn't until the morning of the third day I started to feel damn near invisible. He wasn't talking much, really sad, and so focused. One of those moods where you think so much you over think yourself. You think, then you rethink what you just thought, then you rethink your rethought thoughts. You know what I'm saying; you end up thinking your way out of a damn good thing. He was just a mess.

I was so worried about him because he was worried beyond just recovering from surgery. Something else was on his mind but he hadn't opened up to me about it. I called Porsha to help ease my mind and asked her what she thought it was. She says "He's probably just sad or something you know men, put on something sexy and dance for him he'll cheer up!" I knew that to be true for some men but not Chicago and that's nothing I'd ever do anyway. He was so serious, like me. When we're down, it's not really anything you can do to get us back to ok. We just get better when we get better. I just wanted him to stay focused on feeling better and reaching full recovery.

One day we went to this restaurant up the street and I just had to let him know, "Baby I need you to cheer up. I flew two flights, four hour travel time, and I don't want to be anywhere else in the world but here with you so I need you to put a smile on that face. I know you have a lot on your mind but I love you and I'm always here for you when you're ready to talk." Then he told me he was worried about work, didn't think surgery would be this bad, and felt like I didn't understand that it was hard. Everybody knows when a man is worried about his money they really don't think straight! I understood but I couldn't tell him that because he wasn't hearing it but I was definitely showing it.

He completely missed the fact I was there to love on him, support him, and take care of him in any way I could. I was there when he needed me, and that's all that mattered. Feeling completely neglected, I hung in there and made the best of it. It wasn't about me, it was about him. One thing I'm not is a selfish person.

Eventually, it started to get to me though so I let him know how I felt, and man he did not like that. He took all of that out on me, talking about two things he knew upfront. All of a sudden he says the age difference and distance bothers him. "You're going to have ages and stages", which I will never forget that line as long as I live, was such bullshit! I'm sitting there thinking to myself, I'm young but nobody said dumb and full of cum. I'm older than his ass mentally.

Then he says that he's really been thinking things through. To me these obstacles as he calls it were irrelevant unless you made them relevant. Plus, he must be really insecure to feel that way so early in the relationship. He can date someone his age living next door and have an entirely different set of issues, my point is there will always be some so be thankful when you get minor ones. All I could think was can we please not rush this and take our time. Where did all this thinking come from, shouldn't he just be focused on his knee?

Age and distance didn't keep us from having what we had, we were happy. I was crazy about him and I believed time would've worked out the distance. I would've moved for us, it really meant that much to me. It wasn't hard for me to make that decision because I wouldn't be giving up anything to do so, and my career wouldn't have been affected by relocation either. By this time my guard was down and I was giving 100%. One thing about me, I don't want pieces so I don't give any, know what I'm saying. You know that song by Toni Braxton called How Many Ways? There it was, I couldn't count all the ways I loved him. That man was good to me ok, you couldn't tell me shit. He had nothing to ever be insecure about. I had no complaints, but here he is predicting the future. Won't commit to a vacation in two months but knows what's going to happen in two years.

I tried to brush it off to show him it was nothing to me, I just wanted to stay in the moment and let it be whatever it is. What happened to that? Usually, women rush things, not men! I know all about the settling down, slowing down, and being set in your ways as you get older, but that is what I like in a man. It may not work for everybody else but it works for me. I'm a woman who knows what she wants, and I am very committed to that. To be indecisive is not in me. I'm not a right now, I'm a forever!

Since that conversation he completely ruined everything. When I left he gave me this pathetic hug with the feeling of unsure. He was messed up, my love was gone, and I didn't know what to think about this. Seems like every time you try love it whops out something new on your ass you won't even see coming. I should have listened to my first mind on New Year's Eve. I remembered sitting in the car about to leave on the night we met as he was texting me saying he wanted me to come in so he could give me a proper good bye, blah blah blah. I just thought, "Here we go again." And four months later I was right. All the way home I thought "What the hell just happened?" I couldn't stop trying to figure it out because I didn't understand. What exactly was going on?

We were just loving on each other, missing each other, smiles so big you'd have thought we won the lottery or something and he just destroyed it, just like that, like it never happened. I had no idea how to react. I figured let him come out of it, surgery is probably getting to him. I played it off trying to be reasonable, realizing we all go through stuff sometimes so I'm not going to take it personal.

I felt like he was making problems when we had none. But that ages and stages shit, now that was personal. If I really wanted to go there I'd remind him that only one of us just had a birthday, that's him. And it sounds like he's the one going through some fucking stages! Who I was, what I was giving, and what I wanted from our relationship, had not changed and never would. From that point on his rationality just got more and more pathetic. Then it was, "The thunder came when I was thinking of you and it must be a sign, statistically I just don't think it's going to be successful", blah blah blah.

Every time he talked about it, I became increasingly angry and hurt because he wasn't being a man about it. I'm thinking "Fool, make some fucking sense!" He was looking for reasons to sabotage a good thing because he was scared, he wasn't ready. Don't make me feel like this shit is me when it's you. Finally, once I put my anger aside, sick of texting and talking, fuck all that. I needed to see him face to face so I offered to meet him half way or just come there but he was trying to avoid it so I asked "Why don't you want to see me?" He says "I'm scared to see you because I don't know what's going to happen." I said "Why, what are you so scared of?" He said "Falling in love." I asked why again, and he goes "Because I was falling then."

My reaction is, what did he think was going to happen? We were popping firecrackers and exploding with grins and giggles just looking at each other! Did I miss something? I was under the impression when you have something like that love is oh, somewhere hanging around. To be quite honest, I believe he was already in love and just didn't want to be. What was the problem, it's not like I didn't love him in return. I know, he has issues but I wasn't judging. I have my own and was just hoping he wouldn't become one of them.

But I heard him, he's scared. He says chemistry isn't everything, and I'm saying, "You have everything else, are you blind?" He says he saw a different side of me since his withdrawal from the relationship. Why do men always think when a woman is hurt and angry that it's a "side" of her? It's not some damn "side"; it's her reacting to your actions. It's an emotion, we are both human, in that case you would have a different side of you too if I fed you some bullshit with icing on it and expected you to eat it. Do me a favor, don't fuck up and you won't have to see no damn sides! Matter of fact, I was just up there looking at 3, 4, 5, new sides of him and you didn't see me complaining; I guess I should have been. He didn't even apologize! My grandmother always told me men do what they want and just want you to deal with it. This was the perfect example. It's almost as if he expected me to not be bothered or upset by it. If I care about you how the hell you think I'm going to feel? I just said ok, I'll back off and give him some time to get his head together.

After a few months, a lot of frustration and hurt trying to let him know he had nothing to be scared of, I realized he could not comprehend and digest anything I was saying. I'm a woman and he made it clear in his actions that he's not only used to females, but that's what he wants. That thunder shit must have worked on somebody before me for him to say that like it was acceptable. So is there someone else and he doesn't know how to be upfront with me? What's really going on? He was complaining with such conviction I had to take a step back and say hold up, did I do something? Is there something wrong with me? I'm intelligent, sexy, loyal, ambitious, independent, loving, committed, and giving. I can go on and on about my pros and he sitting up here trying to find some damn cons. He even told me I was a good woman, but that's not what you want? OOOOOKAY!

What 44 year old man doesn't want a fine ass young woman who don't want him for nothing but hugs, kisses, some powerful love making, and a damn good breakfast in the morning before she go make that money! Excuse me, did I say how much I loved to eat! I couldn't believe it, dude was really tripping. The more we talked he was just gone; mind was so far in the clouds you couldn't catch it on a hot air balloon. Like most men, pretty good in everything else but a complete idiot when it comes to a good woman standing in front of their face. I hope he wasn't listening to friends because everybody doesn't want to see you happy. And every man his age is certainly not going to encourage you to be with something they can't get themselves!

It became apparent that he knows females, he doesn't know women. Unfortunately, doesn't know there is a difference. He says there's always women willing to love a man and obviously not seeing why they're so willing…..silly rabbit those are females. You don't have options, you got tricks! All he had to do was say I'm not ready or there's someone else. Just tell me the truth, I would've respected that. I'm not one of those women who can't handle it, I wanted it and damn it I wanted it now. I can't accept bullshit that doesn't make any damn sense. I will keep digging until I find what does make sense. Whatever it was, he didn't want to tell me because he didn't want to close a door he might want to open later.

I thought maybe he was still hurting from divorce and that definitely wouldn't help the situation. People always bring their past experiences into new relationships no matter how much we try to avoid it. I've had horrible experiences but I never, ever, made him pay for someone's past mistakes or subjected him to the repetition of my own.

Life teaches us lessons that we attempt to learn from but sometimes we take it a little too far. I can see tripping over the age difference if I was a young woman who wanted to get married, have kids, and all that but I didn't. I really have no desire to be married, feeling as though I don't need a name change to define my level of commitment. It was there before the piece of paper and would remain after the piece of paper, so what's the purpose? And I don't want any more kids. I have a beautiful baby boy that I will love unconditionally forever, so one is enough for me. The only thing missing in my life was him. I knew it because I missed him every single day since everything happened.

Finally, I came to the conclusion this just isn't working. I can't hang on to something he's not hanging on to. Does it hurt? Absolutely, but I need a man who knows what he wants. This man had no idea. I wanted equal effort and he wasn't giving it so I started asking God to change my heart. Now you may ask yourself, why was I holding on so? Truth is we had all the good stuff made for a successful relationship which is hard to find. I'd be a dumb ass not to hold on. That was once in a life time chemistry and forever was well within our grasp. I loved him naturally and there was nothing I wouldn't do for him. Life is full of ups and downs but one who loves you is consistent and that's what I was. When you go through, those who love you go through too. I noticed we were both doing the same thing, responding by what we felt was said and not what was said. This is what happens when you text and don't speak face to face. Now I had no problem taking the trip to get this done and out of the way, but he would not face me. Honestly, I don't think he can look me in the eyes and say all that smack he was talking because he already know what it is when we are around each other.

I don't believe either of us could look at one another and say anything hurtful because we were really too close for that. I mean, we were tight y'all, if we weren't talking we were sleep! There were boundaries and significant levels of respect especially when it comes to touchy subjects, which was great for the relationship. Still, he made no sense and had horrible communication. I get it, he's a man. He's keeping the poker face and couldn't just tell me how he really felt. Me on the other hand, I'm a woman who speaks her mind and am very passionate about those I love. Don't mess with my son, my money, and my man. My middle name is not game play. He never had to wonder what I was thinking because I told him. The more he kept protecting his self and trying to act like he was protecting me, the more it pissed me off. I'll tell you one thing though, I don't give a damn who he dates, marries, or sleeps with because at the end of the day there's one thing that FEMALE can't and will never be, ME!

After the break up I had to wake up. Chicago was a dream I really wish I never had. I felt the need to get tougher and more prepared for the boomerangs love was going to throw at me in life if I was going to keep trying love. Thinking I couldn't let a man's actions affect me the way this did. Truth is that's all life does, affect you. My emotions were something men don't really understand about women, when we love, we really love. It will be sometime before I begin dating someone new. I'll probably wait even longer than I did the last time. I knew we would never have what we had with each other, with someone else and I was so disappointed.

The usual stay busy and keep your mind going didn't help me stop thinking about him at all. Once my days settled down and my mind was clear, there he was, on it like he'd never left. The time took me through all the phases of happy, sad, and damn it's all bad. But I hung in there and really used that time to reflect on a lot of things within myself, my experiences, and the situations I observe today. I did my best not to become bitter and hate him but instead accept it for what it was…..nothing. I was merely just a good time. I know he would say, "That's not what I meant and that's not what I said." But really, that's how he made me feel and that's how he treated it. He left it like it was nothing so that means it's what? NOTHING! I hate how men try to tell you different than what they actually do, as if you're going to believe their words over their actions. See I was trying to be tough right, but deep down I knew it wasn't really nothing. I was just trying to make sense of what didn't. So, I began to wonder what makes a woman stand out from all the rest. Funny thing is if I'd been a female and left his ass when he was all down and out we'd be having a totally different conversation about how messed up that would've been. But I gave him the opposite and it clearly didn't matter. I decided to take Porsha up on her offer to go out and try a few clubs. I really needed to relax and have a good time so hey, why not? And it was most definitely a new experience. She can tell you all about that.

On the way there we stopped to take some pictures and my silly ass was snapping all kinds of funny poses. But when I tried to get Desire in some funny moments she would just give me this regular old smile. You know the kind that says I really don't want to. I said "Say cheese", and she would just smile. After a few attempts I surprised her and said "Chicagooooo", and boy she was smiling from the inside out. I'll put it this way, that picture was so bright I didn't even need the flash! After that, I took her to this little hole in the wall and it's just that, a hole in the damn wall. I knew a few people on the way in so I stopped and had some words but home girl was really checking the place out. Keeping her hands to herself like she didn't want to come out itching! We found some seats but soon as I sat down I got up and started dancing immediately.

This was one of those places that everybody and they mama has a good time. These men have nothing to lose and they'll ask anyone to dance regardless of how they look. The females that come are of all ages and either let it all hang out or try to suck it all in. You can just imagine how much Desire & I stood out. Like two big diamonds in a pile of rocks, we were the furthest from fitting in.

I was dancing with this old man, that old man, and this young man. All were every bit of broke, funky, stank breath, rotted teeth, and a hard on! Desire cracked me up though. Every time I sat down she gave me some hand sanitizer and said "Get the bacteria off, it kills 99.9% of germs!" Anybody that watched her had to laugh too. This was the most I'd ever seen her laugh since we met. She sat there the entire time all reserved and up tight with her mind in another world. But to everyone's surprise the DJ put on J.Cole Power Trip, and she flew out of that chair.

All the men on the dance floor were trying to get behind her and everyone was watching her but you could see in her eyes she was missing Chicago. Girlfriend put her drink in the air and started singing "Would you believe me if I said I'm in love….." She said she on one and I didn't even think she knew what the hell one was but she was having fun! And it really went down once they put on TGT Sex Aint Never Felt Better!!!! The DJ was truly playing to keep her dancing. The men in there didn't have a chance with Desire but they tried anyways. She's not one that needs to take her clothes off to get the rooms attention. Some guys leaned over and ask me "What's up with her, she got a man? It looks like she's thinking about somebody?" I said "Yeah, some punk ass named Chicago!" He said "Well, I don't know where the hell dude is at but he damn sure missing out, everything on her fine ass is real, DAMN!" Only in this type of joint would somebody say something like that.

I asked her what was on her mind and she said "I'm starting to wonder if men do this kind of stuff on purpose? Would they really rather share a relationship with a female who cannot love them equally but wants their financial stability in return for sex? Has society really become a sell yourself or you will never find yourself with someone else? He got what he wanted Porsha, that's all that matters to him. I wasn't nothing special, he just made me feel that way to get what he wanted and he got it. Joke is on me. I'm the one out here feeling five miles to empty, not him! All that other shit was for the birds, he meant none of it. Fuck you, hurt you, and kick your ass to the curb is the name of the game. It's fuck or be fucked out here and I got fucked up."

I totally understood where she was coming from but I had no answers for baby girl. Her mind was telling her that but her heart wasn't. The shit was crazy but she was tough and really took it like a woman. Sucked it up and was determined to get better. When we left we stopped through the Jazz District to see if it was hitting that night. I was surprised Desire hadn't said she was ready to go home yet, it was well past her bedtime and I know she loves to sleep. She's a true Leo, loves to eat and sleep. Don't disturb her because if you make her get up she'll make you wish you hadn't. I was worried for her because she was so hurt and frustrated but I kept thinking if that was me I would've been in Chicago cursing that fool out at his house. Not her though, she was a real charge it to the game type of chick so that wasn't her style. As we were strolling down the street this guy named Vincent stopped me to talk. I could tell Desire didn't like him from the get go but I wasn't turning down any possibilities.

What else is new, I try to remain open for love but men skip over me so fast never realizing I'm the jackpot. I went ahead and asked him how old he was and he stuttered for a second. Before he could attempt at giving me his age again Desire jumped in like sister knows best, "She's trying to make sure you meet the credentials and your stuttering was the first sign of lying." I told you she does not play. He proceeded to play it off and said he was 42 but looked every bit of 56. Tired and ready to go home, I skipped entertaining the conversation and we exchanged numbers. We shared a few phone conversations and he offered to take me out one evening for BBQ. I got all ready, hot and sexy just how I like to be. On the way there, I focused my mind on being positive and not going in with a negative outlook. You know the whole give him a chance crap. I arrived first and he pulled up in his Lexus a few minutes later. We went in and ordered but this lady came over and said she would show me where he usually likes to sit. Until I mentioned it to Desire, I didn't even think that to be a little fishy but it seemed like he knew everyone in there. I wasn't exactly fond of having BBQ for a first date but that's what I wanted. I sent Desire a text and turns out she was on her way up there.

I didn't even see her come in and get any food but she wrote back and said "Girl, if you want my opinion the answer is NO to everything. Matter of fact, HELL NO! And that's not a Lexus, that's an old ass car on rims!" We shared different standards but hoped for the same thing when it came to relationships. He started to grow on me and I felt some attraction to him. That was really important to me, having a man I was physically attracted to. We left there and went out to play pool which I happened to know a thing or two about. I thought it was cute he assumed I knew nothing and proceeded to try to teach me something. A few games later we decided to call it a night and I thought a second date was in order. After all, I did have a good time so invited him over one evening for dinner and he pulled a no call no show. Yes, I'm talking about this like a job because that's just what dating is these days. I decided he's getting two weeks of my time. Let the clock start ticking because I could already tell he was just like all the rest.

If you're not putting out in the first week they don't hear anything you say or have any interest after. See the last man I dated a while back got a year of my life and nothing more. After that experience I'm down to two weeks, enough said. The second time I invited him over he did it again but this time said he fell asleep. I'm thinking he's got two strikes and we're not even one week in. As we continued to talk I noticed our schedules were off so we really couldn't spend any time together. By the time I got home from work he was already settled in the bed so I attempted one more time when we had the same off day. We had planned to spend the day together working out and taking a trip to the zoo. The day comes and dude shows up trying to do this weak ass work out. I had that fool lifting weights once he was finished lolly gagging! See I work out every other day; I keep this body fit right and very tight. After an hour or so he says he's going to run home to shower and come back for the zoo. I said ok but two hours later there was still no Vincent. Just like a man, want you sitting around waiting on their ass.

Of course, he never showed. Now I let the first time slide but was sure to text him after the second time he stood me up letting him know I don't play games. Desire always told me to watch the things they don't respond to, and guess what, he never responded to that. But he stands me up the third time and continues to call as if nothing ever happened. I had waited so long after my last long term relationship to date again only to find out men haven't changed. Their sorry asses are still the same and maybe even worse. I start dating again only to see it's the same shit just a different asshole! That was enough for me so I decided I don't even want a relationship. At least back in the day dating lasted a few months; this dumb ass didn't even make it two weeks. His excuses of getting a haircut at 11 o'clock at night, dropping off pizza to kids on a week day but said he only has them on weekends, and his mother's birthday was on the day we had planned together yet he act like he didn't know about it in advance was straight up weak!

At that age his game should've been smooth as hell. That let me know he's used to dealing with what, FEMALES, and their dumb asses don't care as long as they are getting some money. Desire told me she thought he was living with someone either his wife or the mother of his kids since I'd ask him to come through and he would say "We'll see." Meaning, I'll be there if I can get out of where I'm supposed to be. That was good enough for me, so another long break from dating it is! That was such a waist of my time and thoughts, so I put his ass on block. Funny when you do that they blow up your phone!

I went by Desire's house for a girls' night and told her about it. She was in one of her cooking moods and I never miss those opportunities. You'll put on 10 lbs when you leave her kitchen. I said, "I just don't get it girl. We're beautiful women, not complaining, bitching, asking for money, and all that other crap but we get done like this. Ungrateful ass men make me sick. I'm not about to keep trying love, I'd rather be alone because this is so exhausting." I was just going on and on about men and then I realized I kept hearing myself. I paused and looked over at her snapping green beans as tears were welling in her eyes. I said, "Baby girl are you ok?" "Yes, yes I'm fine." she said. But I knew she wasn't, her face was stone and she looked like she was trying not to let a single tear drop. I'd forgotten if you say love around that girl she just gets silent. It reminds her of

Chicago and these days she's on the impossible mission to forget his existence. If only all women had that gift the world would be a much better place. I wanted to tell her that she can't and it was a waste of time but I didn't want to see her break. That would've struck a nerve for real, I know because I've been there before. We both sat there looking at each other like what the hell? I knew we couldn't be the only women tired of this shit. Vincent was playing my ass off and treating me like I was some female, Chicago did her the same damn way. They always leave good women for the trash. I'm telling you, good men don't want good women.

Eight Months Later…………………….

EXPOSED

Chicago and I always kept in touch, trying to remain just friends I guess. We texted often and regardless of my feelings, it seemed to be going alright. Every now and then I'd express to him what was going through not only my mind but my heart as well, on the days I missed him most. We would talk about what happened sometimes but I tried to avoid it, I didn't feel like it was a deal breaker I just felt it was really stupid. He just couldn't get over the distance and I was done trying to make him feel better about it so not much changed. I know I know, why in the world would I still have any feelings for that fool but first of all let me tell you something. Can't nobody, and I mean nobody, talk about my love but me. Second, nobody totally understands your feelings but you and what it's like to deal with them every day. Third, I'd been praying and waiting for God to change my heart. I tried everything I could to stop loving someone I felt didn't love me. I just gave up and accepted that I'll feel this way until my heart says otherwise. If you keep running from something you'll eventually run to it, so I let it be. In his words, I stand strong that he was the right path he just merely veered from it. See this is exactly why I don't like to feel shit. Yes, I still had no answers to what happened. What changed so for him to be unsure of something that is certain? But on this very day I was about to find out the truth.

Spring is over, summer came, fall is gone, and winter is here. Thanksgiving passed and now I'm twenty days from Christmas. I had just taken a trip to Chicago on business and went by to see him as I hadn't heard from him and that's not like him. He always text me even if

it's just to say he's doing fine so I knew something was
wrong. I was very worried and I was right. When I
arrived he told me he had a family emergency, was been
busy with his son and with school. I just said alright. I
had no expectations but Lord knows I would be crushed
if anything had happened to him.

I told him where I was staying and he said he'd come by
after some plans with his son but he ended up keeping
him overnight and didn't make it. The next day I saw
him and as usual, he was studying and told me he's been
trying not to get distracted. He was really focused on
getting school out of the way by next year and I couldn't
get mad at him for pushing toward accomplishments. I
must say, I am a little bit of a distraction looking this
good! We shared what was going on, how my trip was
going, and all the usual stuff. A few minutes turned into
over an hour. I was very proud of him and I supported
him no matter what he wanted to do in life. Friends or
not, he was cool people. I gave him a few tips for school
and a big hug; then smiled back at him smiling at me as

he did in February. He was smiling so hard you could see all 32 of his teeth! After all that time, fireworks were still there. We exchanged text for a while as I was on my way to my next stop. I was sure to let him know when I made it home safely. It is hard to go to school and be in a relationship, but we weren't in one so I wasn't tripping.

I asked if he misses me and he always says the same answer, "Yes, stop fishing." I can't help it, I just hoped he'd have a little faith, realize I wouldn't do anything to hurt him and come around sometime. I really missed him. I asked him several times on several different occasions if he had started dating or seeing someone because I felt like he was acting kind of funny. But he never mentioned it just said he's on the usual work, school, charity program, etc. We were kind of going back and forth about Christmas presents and I couldn't figure out what to get him if anything at all. As I was shopping around though I had found so much I wanted to send him anyway and I figured it's Christmas, I have *to get my love something. I found these blue tooth ear warmers that would've been great for him at work whenever he has to be out in the cold. Then I saw these nice house shoes, I bought myself a pair too, and they would've been great for his knee as well so I sent him a text telling him what I found and asked him about his shoe size. He had just text me back and said it depends and I told him I wouldn't tell him what kind they were.*

A moment later, it seemed as though someone was texting me from his phone. They asked, "Who is this?" I said "Wrong person Love"; before I knew it I was receiving some serious bullshit. Some "female" was on the other end talking about how my number wasn't saved. It was an out of state area code so I must be pretty irrelevant. It's northwestern Missouri, I'm texting pretty far and she hopes it was worth it. She's his woman and she's in his bed waiting on him to get out the shower. I told her "Get back to your friend you don't want none bye." She proceeds to go on and on saying how she's grown and she don't take kindly to BS, that I need to delete the number, and have sweet dreams. First of all, the bitch must've had an idea of who I am to say what she said about out of town and pretty irrelevant. Meaning, he or someone else has told her about his long distance relationship. Her ratchet ass didn't realize she wasn't shit because I sure didn't know about her, and why would he need to lie to me? Who the fuck is irrelevant now bitch! And why would you tell another grown woman that you are grown unless you felt like she wasn't. She knew what she was doing but she was barking up the wrong tree. Batty better ask somebody!

I'm generally a calm person for those I care about and I don't fight no bitch over a dick, but this one better not see me! She made this personal. I realized quick she's one of them hos that delete the text and then fuck him to change his perspective before she says anything about it because men are even dumber after sex than they were before it. Pussy blocks brains! Everything with females is deception and control. A chess game if you will; and a man will never win unless he has a woman to tell him the real deal. We can tell you what she's going to do next, why, and how to get 10 steps ahead of her ass. The ironic thing about it is he went in on me about maturity; ages and stages but he has a grown ass "female" not a woman, texting me from his damn phone trying to hurt my feelings like we're in the 2nd grade. Who the fuck is going through ages and stages now mother fucker?!!! Mature on that!

It is one thing to be going through a phone but it's a whole different ball game when you're bold enough to text the woman in his phone from his own phone! Now that's a female! If she was a woman I wouldn't have ever heard from her, she would've been talking to him and only him. Since when does a man who claims to date nothing but fine women, who are the shit, sleep with a bimbo who goes through cell phones. PLEASE! That bitch was trying to come up missing, I'd been having one hell of a year and she messed with me at the wrong damn time. And she's not "the" shit, she is shit!

He clearly doesn't know what "the" shit is but he's about to find out. And I already know she's sitting up somewhere trying to make something that aint there! I said nothing that night but trust there was no sleep and nothing but tears. Tears of frustration because I've asked him several times was he seeing anybody and he never said anything about it so hint to that ho, she wasn't important. If she was none of this would've happened. I was the real thing, long distance, but he will never find another and this confirmed he knew it. She was the local booty and well, men are visual creatures. Not that I'm saying she's much to look at.

So then it all came together, the thunder, how the distance was hard, bullshit bullshit bullshit. It was a female! This fool put me on a shelf for a ratchet. Who parks a Maserati to lease a Pontiac? Temp bitches get on my damn nerves! No wonder he said stop fishing, he didn't want me to find out his ass was catching bottom feeders! Didn't he just finish re-establishing and starting over after a divorce, dumb ass hadn't learned shit! If he was stupid enough to do this, he was stupid enough to wife the bimbo he was sleeping with. I wonder what kind of sign he'll get when the thunder sounds again. There'll be a rain storm every day soon, spring is on the way! Funny thought, doesn't it always rain on weddings and funerals? I think if we all read that as a sign of hesitation there would be a lot less divorce rates!

Females play games much like most men, there's just a different objective and Batty B was making her next move. See one thing about a woman is, we know what females do but we are too damn good to play dirty. She basically figured she was going to fuck him until he forgets me or anybody else for that matter. Her responses to me not only proved that she felt threatened but as a female her plan was to get rid of options. Bitch don't realize that she ended up making a decision for him that he really wasn't ready to make and he will resent her if not cancel that ho for pulling that little stunt whether he'll admit it or not. Bitch will be gone soon as the warm weather breaks! You never mess up a man's game. Now what really takes the cake is the next morning. I called him before he went to work and left him a message that I needed to talk to him as I was really upset. At this point, I don't know if it will get to him or the bimbo so I sent a text and said I was on my way. A few moments later he said, "Hell no!!! This is where we cease communication". I WENT THE FUCK OFF!!!!!!!!

Now I know damn well this fool don't want me to come to the Chi and get it cracking because I will most definitely set it off! Why respond like that unless you knew you were wrong? I told him," You don't want none of this so just tell the truth and I won't come up there because if I do, it will certainly be unforgettable and fucking EPIC! Think I'm playing!" It was so stupid to lie about it or even decided as just friends that he wants to end all communication. OH HELL NO! I didn't start this shit he did, back when he gave me that sorry ass excuse he pulled out of a fucking story book. This fool tried Reading Rainbow on my ass and said "The thunder came *when I was thinking about you and that must be a sign..." PLEASE! I've been going months trying to deal with this shit because he could've at least stuck to the script. Don't just act like a man mother fucker BE ONE! If you want to fuck bitches, say that. If you don't want everything but you want extra, say that. If I was nothing special, just a good time, say that. Own that shit! Don't avoid the truth because you don't want to admit how much of an asshole you are and don't bullshit me like I'm a fucking idiot! He was trying that whole let her down easy crap but being who I am, I can't process bullshit and I don't translate it either. Don't try to tell me something without telling me. It's as if he was trying to communicate on a level he thought I was on and would understand but my level is where his should have been!*

He should have and could have been straight up with me, kept it 100, and said what he was so confused or torn about. He can't even deny what's real, like I said before, he know what it is. Remember when I said I was trying to be tough and talk like it was nothing, well it was something, and I was hanging on. For him to hide the fact he was seeing somebody, he was too. But as usual they never want what's effortless. If they can't play a game with you they don't want you. If he had no intentions on trying to do anything outside of a friendship with me he would have told my ass he was seeing someone since we were just friends. He had messed up months ago, what was the big deal about keeping Batty B a secret from me. Hell, I told him when I was trying to start dating. Keyword, trying! The million dollar question is what did he have to lose by telling me the truth, other than me? Seriously, what did his sorry ass have to lose? If I didn't mean anything why hide it from me?

Oh, but now that I knew he was hitting more than just the books he didn't have anything to say. There's nothing like feeling wrong when you thought your ass was right! "I haven't had any free time since I started school." Everything he'd said echoed in my head relentlessly, I laughed so hard I could've broke a rib! So I *guess we didn't have anything to talk about since my love turned out to be an asshole. Now that I knew the thunder meant, I don't have a reason and can't find a reason to leave you but I just have to mess up a good thing because if I don't it will last forever. Thinking things through meant, let me put you on hold while I try this one out and then I'll know what I want to do. His problem was I wasn't waiting on that bullshit. And that maturity line meant let me do you however I want to do you and I expect you not to say anything. Oh no, being with me was too easy, just made too much sense, that would just be too much like right!*

They always leave you alone once they can't lie to you. It's almost as if it takes the joy out of their game. How the hell you're a grown ass 44 year old man with a game so sloppy you get caught LONG DISTANCE because you're sleeping with a "female". Come on now, that was just pathetic. And to make matters worse, he had a beautiful young woman that loved him whole heartedly. No amount of money in the world could've made me hurt him, and he pushed that to the side for some ratchet acting 18! I'm not about to babysit no grown ass man. I can't believe she nursing his little phone trying to eliminate what she feels is a potential threat. I take that back, I can believe it since she was texting me like a female, that's what bat shit bitches do. He didn't understand what she was really doing let alone what he just did to his-self.

I knew that thunder shit was for the birds, what really happened? No man is going to leave a beautiful woman long distance or not to be alone. Men are never alone! Had he been upfront then, he wouldn't be looking like a dumb ass now. And since we're just friends and you supposedly have no feelings, what you stop talking to me for. He stopped talking to me like he was trying not to mess up shit with Batty B. Or the usual, that's too much to make up for so now I really have to keep it moving. I didn't do anything to him, he better check that female! I didn't say shit to that bitch, she came for this. Trust and believe if devastation had not hit me first, she was definitely going to get it. That five hour drive was about to be two!

Hell, I figured she's a bat shit bitch, he was acting like a punk ass bitch, sounded like a match. I hope they fuck until they fucking self-destruct! Don't let the youth fool you, I know all the old tricks and was about to teach them both a little of the new. But back to him, he thinks he's just going to send me that shit because he's busted. Don't act like it if you're not because we hadn't been together in months. He was trying to keep up this persona for me and she tore it down. She exposed his punk ass. See if he was the player he was trying to be, he could've gotten a better outcome if he played his cards right but remember, I said I loved him. I never said he was smart!

That fool could've said "I wasn't ready to tell you, didn't know how to or if I should", or even just a plain, "That wasn't cool and I didn't mean for you to find out like that". Hell anything but he chose to treat me like I did something wrong. I didn't deserve that shit. If he wanted to get off that easy he better date some cougars so old they have no spark left to kick his ass. I text that fool 20 times and said EVERYTHING I needed to say but I'm not done with his ass. Oh no, I'm NOT DONE! Trust me he may not feel shit but pussy as he is a man but he definitely thought about how sloppy shit was. I know the females would say, "Girl you could've had him if you just played the game", I'm not about to do all of that. I don't need to trick no mother fucker into giving me a ring! When you do that, your ride doesn't last that long. He was playing games and he found Batty to play with him. I wasn't playing games for a reason, it wouldn't be fair, if I get on the board there will be no competition!

Now why in the hell at his age would you ever set your-self up for failure and receive some bad karma because you couldn't find the balls to rectify a mistake? I was surely bout to bring my own pair and help him find his when I got up there. He must be crazy to think he's going to run from this, oh no, his bitch ass is going to feel this shit. Believe that! When I said it he probably thought I meant physically but first of all, I'm not going to jail or hell for anybody! And secondly, he can go to the doctor for all that physical shit, I meant he was going to feel this mentally and emotionally, just....like.....me! There's nothing a drug or doctor can give you for what I was about to give his ass.

I remembered telling him in the beginning I didn't need any more damage than I already had and if he was playing games or just wanted sex to keep it moving because I wasn't with it. If he was looking for love I didn't have that much of a heart left to give him any and that was going to take some time but if he was good to me I'd always be great to him. That asshole says "You're selling yourself short; I hope to mend some of those wounds, blah blah blah." This mother fucker tried to teach me a lesson I already learned, but oooooohhhhh look who's learning now ass hole!

I wasn't upset about the bimbo, hell I knew he was sleeping with somebody; I was upset about not telling me. All this time he just let me continue to hurt over what happened, I could've been done letting that go had he been a grown ass man and told the truth. He wasn't keeping it from me because of my feelings, it was because of his. He knew what he was to me and part of him wanted it to stay that way, selfish mother fucker! Whenever a man knows he's going to have to step up they always step their punk ass down! This is the idiot that preached to me about maturity but his ass is silent! Where was he going, oh no, he better bring his grown ass back here and get this grown ass whooping! A mature man would've owned his shit regardless of how bad it stunk, not ran from it like a little punk! If he was trying to keep his player card on deck his game should've been tighter than a 16 year old virgin messing around with me. Nooooo, he's keeping my ass in the background while he's fucking with Batty in the foreground!

He must have been really insecure about his-self to be putting notches on a belt like he's a teenage boy. I tell these fools all the time, if you can't afford a Maserati get your ass off the LOT! Even though I was trying to be tough, I laughed and cried until my tear ducts dried. By the way, some of this may sound like I'm conceded and feeling myself but when a man does you like this, you better remind yourself who you are! If you don't you will lose yourself and that's exactly what they want. That's how you end up being weak, losing respect for yourself, and making mistakes you'll forever regret. I was so disgusted with the thought of him sleeping with some ratchet I took the longest shower in history. I couldn't believe he played me for the local booty! All the love I had for him and all he wanted was pussy. I wanted to cut that shit out and throw it at him. Hell men can have it, take it, I don't want it if this is what it comes with it. I'd gotten a hell of a lot more pain than pleasure from it so they can keep it. Some of you may say that's a little extreme but ladies just be honest, it can get like that sometime. The sad part about it is this is where men always, and I do mean always, mess up. They always go left when they should've gone right. I told him that bimbo was about to serve him up something decent because that's what her type does.

Funny after all this time looking at myself and searching for understanding, I have wasted every minute of it. Here I was trying to recover from the emotional damage relationships have caused me, going to therapy, taking anti-depressants to have more good days than bad, just trying to become a better person to meet someone who'll love me in return. I wouldn't wish it on my worst enemy to love someone that doesn't love you. Aside from funerals, it's the most painful thing I've experienced. Some wouldn't agree with that but look, they have pain killers for everything else! I was trying not to let his fucked up actions and that of others, change me into a bitter bitch. I was just trying to maintain. You know, trying to keep it together. I am so sick of love always putting my ass through some damn changes.

This wasn't all about him; he was just the icing on the cake. I did everything I was supposed to including giving him the benefit of the doubt and this is what I got. Fuck love, marriage, and men! Until death do us part my ass, more like until death am I done! I'm tired of how it's always something wrong with the woman when a relationship ends. It's never anything wrong with a man because they live by the true definition of find them, fuck them, and forget them. My response is, when he fucks you up, FUCK HIM UP! And if you need some ideas, give a sister a call! I'll give them something they've never had before! This jerk didn't do me any favors but I'm supposed to do him one and walk away, you're kidding right?! I'm tired of giving these punk ass mother fuckers what they're not giving me! I'm not about to stick to the script and say, "I'll be alright, I just wasn't the one for him, there must be someone better for me, he didn't deserve me, and you win some you lose some."

WHATEVER! To hell with that let it go, move on, and get over it shit! Not this time, oh no, not this time. If a man said that to me right now I'd probably castrate his ass!

I'll be damn if another man makes a fool out of me. Women are always left picking up the pieces and trying to get control of something we can't even see or touch, feelings! Fuck feelings! Punk asses like him don't feel shit, if they did they wouldn't be fucking someone else the next day, hell or even the same night they left your ass. What, I'm supposed to say everybody deals with things differently. Yes that's true, but not that damn different! Truth is men don't put anything into the relationship to begin with, that's why they move on so quickly. You can do that when you have no losses. Now you may think that's just too much, but life will do that to you. Don't judge my efforts, if someone you felt some type of way about told you some crap like what he told me, it would mess you up too! At least I was addressing my issues and trying to better myself, don't matter how I was trying to do it. I'm not ashamed of my story or my struggle, just like that asshole says, "It is what it is!"

Some of the things he said had me doubting myself and if men saw me as I see me. To tell the truth, if enough people treat you the same way you'll start to believe them, don't matter how you feel about yourself. I had started to think maybe I wasn't this, I wasn't that, I wasn't, I wasn't, I wasn't. Get the point! Then something in me reminded me who the hell I was and told me to remind his ass too. And to those who read this and say, sounds like she hasn't been through nothing to love him that much and to go through all of that. Let me tell you something, I've been through it, up it, down it, and around it. I learned to let my feelings come naturally. This was so right everything else before it was wrong! That's how I knew he was the right path, but just because a woman knows it doesn't always mean a man knows it. They usually realize it when it's too late. Somewhere after that karma hits them from what they did to the good woman and then they want to go back.

Yes, I understand there are much worse experiences which I've had my share of but will not be discussing. If I did you would be reading for the next 5 years. Let's just say, I shouldn't have to go through hell to get to heaven. God didn't say anything about all that!

I'm not going to keep kissing frogs to get a prince and if you believe that, you're tripping. Men think I'm supposed to play dumb, think they're different, let them get a piece of me and throw me back in the sea so another one can catch me and do the same thing, that's funny! The now, the new, and the next are not about to be running through me until I hit some bullshit man lottery and meet one at the time he wants to settle down. HELL NAW!

I'm sure reading this you feel sorry for me and what I went through but DON'T. Feel sorry for him, I'll be alright. He won't! They always say hell hath no fury like a woman scorned, you notice they never say that about a man. I wonder why that is? I admire a lot of traits in men and I'm not talking about dipping their sticks in more than one dip at a time. I try to learn from them to be able to date and actually handle anything to come my way. I try to take the best of both worlds. Fuck that fairy tale shit. I know that does not exist.

By the end of everything that happened I thought how much I hated being a woman sometimes. I'm putting in all this work, prayer, and pills but this fool just fucks a new one and moves right along like nothing ever happened. I was beyond pissed. I wanted to Tyson that ass! I know you're thinking "Damn, was it that bad?" Yes, it was that bad because the love was that good, and I'm not talking about sex! The love was so good I know beyond any reasonable doubt that what he got is not better! I always said its fuck or get fucked and man I give him the best fucker award because he definitely screwed me over and then some. He put some of the highest paid actors to shame. All of that wasn't even necessary. He was heartless, numb, cold, and all the other stuff I wish I could be every now and then to survive in this world. It makes life so much easier when you can do what he did to me, when you can do what they do all the time. This is exactly why I don't hate on females, I somewhat admire them. They give these punk ass mother fuckers the business they deserve. Women just aren't them and they just aren't women.

Hell, I would high five Batty B because she's about to do her damn job, but I don't touch special breeds! Now most women would detest what I just said but it's just a reality for me so I have to get my ass out the kitchen because I can't take the heat. Hell, I've got third degree burns and beyond messing around with these fools. So what else do you do when love don't love you?

I called my girls to get my mind right but that wasn't helping. I hate talking to everybody else about someone else, but I knew I had to deal with this differently. And it was most definitely going to get dealt with. I called Porsha, "You want me to yank that mother fucker? I'm putting my shoes on, we riding on his bitch ass! You may not want to fuck that bitch up but I got that ratchet for you. How the fuck he think he gone play your ass like that? I know all about y'all and if he didn't tell you about that ho that's because there was nothing to tell. And that punk ass mother fucker thinks he's gone cut you off like you aint shit. Fuck him and every nigga look like him! I know its hard girl but it would be different if you were there, you probably would've been engaged by now. I don't think his intention was to play you really I don't. It's simple she's there and you're not. He'll regret it, they always do. He didn't have to do you like that though. What you want to do? I'm ready, get locked and loaded."

I told her, "It's cool, just give me a few days. I've got a better idea." She said, "Aaaww shit, that mother fucker got you silent! Aaaawww shit, girl what you bout to do because I know you? This runs deep for you, silence is not a good sign for that asshole. Does he know you excel at raising hell?!" I laughed and hung up not wanting to discuss my plans but girlfriend was right. He got the *wrong one. I'm from KC, this is the Show Me State and if you don't know, you're about to! Don't bring it here boo. Porsha's the type that will go postal on a man in a minute. She'll go to their job, their house, their mother's house, their baby's mother's house, and any place else she can find them. Me on the other hand, I like to be a bit more creative!*

So here I was torn between my heart and my mind, waiting for another year to be over again. I went on walks, started routine work outs, tried retail therapy which was hard as hell because I stack, I don't spend. I needed a drink every day to relax my mind from the sleepless nights and restraint from doing just what my girl wanted to do, whoop that ass! I was so disappointed because I really liked him, really loved him. I thought he was just great and it was hard to swallow that I fell in love with who I thought he was, who I knew him to be, and as it turns out that's not him. I kept asking myself, why? As if this bitch was worth it. I get it, I'm on the shelf and she's in the bottom drawer. She's convenient.

He has to reach for me but she's right there, he can just
pull it out and do his thing. I was worth reaching for
though, good things don't come without hard work.
Convenience and laziness doesn't screw others, it screws
you. I know men think he probably had one there and
had me here, it as a controllable situation.

I get it, he thought he could have it all but unfortunately,
HE CAN'T! If that was the case, why waste my time, stay
with that bitch. Don't fuck me over to end up with her
ass, just stay with that. If you want ass on the side go
buy a ho! I'm not your side dish, back burner, or plan B
bitch! FUCK HIM! That's what you use females for and
I'm not no damn female! The only reason you need a
plan B is because you KNOW plan A isn't going to work
out! Men always gravitate to challenges instead of
guarantees. They're always in the street trying to
conquer what they can't. He had everything he could
have possibly wanted and needed in me, nothing was off
limits. Hold up, I meant that within reason! And after
what I've been through in life that says a whole hell of a

lot. I not only was the best, I gave him the best and he's going to do me like this. You can't find another woman on this earth to love him the way I did. There is no other woman like the one he had! What the hell was he thinking? You know what, he wasn't!

I was officially drained emotionally, mentally, and physically. Women always feel that way after their heart is broken but there's a certain point after that. It's the straw that breaks the camel's back and enough was enough. I was so hurt, disappointed, and utterly destroyed more than anything else. I didn't know who to be mad at most, him or me.

I knew this was my fault. I messed up by expecting him to be a man. You know that expect it and you'll receive it crap, never again! FYI, just because they look like one on the outside doesn't mean they are on the inside. I blame myself for believing after previous bad experiences that he was a good one. I was the one acting brand new like I didn't know his ass was going to mess up when I met

him. I lied to myself more than he lied to me. I pretty
much helped him screw me over by trying to be hopeful,
think positive, and give him the opportunity to show me
he was different. I did the leg work and he took the
credit. Men have always shown me that they never want
everything in one woman; they just want one thing from
every woman. I let myself down and I've been struggling
all year trying to live with that. I knew better, I knew
he'd want something else, knew he'd want a female. I
was silly to think I finally met someone who appreciated
what I had to give. Silly to think I met a man who was
ready for a life time.

I realized that I had these expectations for a reason, at
the time he was meeting them. I was receiving what I
was giving, until I wasn't! Turns out he's nothing special,
just a man. Like I said, don't feel shit but what, you
already know. It was never him, it was me all along. I
know that sounds like some sad shit but it's real, it's
what I know. Good for you if you know different. That's
when it dawned on me; part of this is because men don't

know what a good woman is. They always got shit backwards. Do the female thing, and then get a woman when you are ready for one. And if you happen to find a woman while you're doing the female thing, just be straight up about what you have going on. You can't play a game like you own it when you didn't even invent it. OK! Don't try to make a female into a woman. Stop marrying for pussy instead of love, you won't get that far. Brains and beauty can do more for you than breast and booty ever will.

Females and women only have one thing in common; they both take you to the bed and the bank. Females make withdrawals out of yours', and women make deposits into what you have together. In that moment I realized men think we are all alike. Females are like gravity, they're only objection is to bring you down and most of you deserve it. Women only want to love you for love in return. Maybe men do not understand everything with a vagina is not the same. Men don't want me to say they're all the same but they treat women like we're all the same. Maybe they don't know what a woman is or even how to get one. Men like Chicago however, need to ask themselves why the hell they keep passing over blessings to keep learning lessons. Stupid ass was running from the woman that wanted him and running to the female that wanted something from him. They all do it, they don't understand they are good enough for a woman but your money needs to be good enough for a female! Unfortunately, most men never learn so I happen to have the desire to teach them.

Females are not women and women are not females! You can't even compare the two but it seems like men don't realize there's a damn difference. Remember, this is not a man bashing book or even a book to bash females. Men, females can only be who they are because you are who you are. They can't be a ho if you're not screwing them, stupid! If you can't be a man in public at least be one in private. Own your mistakes, grab a drink, sit back, and let me teach you a few things. Men, you put the MEN in MENtally Challenged!

PART II

All Kinds of Females, One Kind of Woman

Okay men, listen up! There are two human beings in this world we call earth that have vaginas, Females & Women. Unfortunately, the longer I keep living the more I find you guys don't know the damn difference. So here is your ultimate break down. This is not by any means written with the intent of clowning females, they are not us and we are not them. Don't make this about them, it's about you! And I mean, all about YOU! Let's start with females and keep it simple.

- Gold Diggers- females who use men for money
- Trap-a-trash- females who intentionally get you locked up or get pregnant on purpose to keep you in their life as long as they want, welcome to the land of the leashes!
- Child support careers- females who have a baby by every man they meet to receive consistent income
- Crazy Hos- females that provide everything you want sexually and are most of the time a side dish but once they see screwing you is not making them number one they SNAP…watch the show (Key words: number one not only one)
- Turkey Baster Bitches- commonly found in the entertainment industry, females use such objects to impregnate

themselves with a man's sperm in hopes of obtaining a constant check or hush money

- Serial divorcers- females constantly re-marrying to divorce or become widows for money. They usually move from state to state, background check needed!

- Filthy Females- they don't keep anything clean; sometimes not even their ass. They are hoarders and just damn nasty! Doesn't mean they don't work, may even have good jobs, but once you see their home please consider what you may be dealing with for the rest of your life. Only thing you can do for them is give them your check and pay their bills!

Now there are plenty of examples of this in real life and on television. I know some men are a little slow when it comes to this but I hope not that slow. Also, please don't think that when a female has kids and makes good money that means something because actually, it means nothing. You must look closer at priorities, changes, and other red flags that may appear. Such as, are they hiding their financial business? Do they want your name on everything and not theirs, play domestic violence games, and beat themselves to say you beat them? Some females have the objective of wanting you to stop taking care of your own kids to take care of theirs by someone else. Yes, you heard right! By the way, only females mess with men they know are in committed relationships and marriages. Females have no respect for themselves or another woman's man. They are direct reflections of most of you! Their asses will sleep with a married man and won't even take the ring off. FYI women do not share any man; they want their own and deserve their own.

There are all types of crazy in the world, just don't act like you didn't see it coming. If you weren't trying to be captain save a ho, you would never have to deal with the ruined credit or violent record you now hold on the account of a female.

There is only one kind of woman in this world. She is intelligent, responsible, accountable, loving, compassionate, loyal, understanding, honest, natural, supportive, sexy, sumptuous, sensual, giving, appreciative, considerate, thoughtful, committed, faithful, reserved, compromising, independent, self-sufficient, creative, a team player, ambitious, God fearing, respectful, classy, sophisticated, educated, career driven, inspiring, spiritual, and mentally stable. She don't take no bullshit, she don't play no games, she's not selfish, she does not have a bunch of kids by different men, she's clean physically and environmentally, healthy, maintains herself, and exercises. If she has kids they are a wonderful reflection of her. If she has a daughter she keeps her hair done before she gets her own done. She is not flamboyant, loud, rude, raunchy, and has no ho tendencies. Last but not least, she is never threatened by or going out of her way to eliminate another woman or female because we don't make them a factor to begin with. I'm sure after the last chapter I don't need to go into what maturity means. We don't do what the ratchets do!

A woman is looking for a man to be on her team! He's family oriented, mentally stable, thoughtful, financially stable, secure, confident, honest, serious when needed, and know how to please a woman in the bed. She's looking for a man that she can trust to be the man at all times, keeping the best interest of her and their family at heart. Some of you just read that and thought it sounds like too much work. Listen, if it's real it's not work!

When a woman loves, she loves unconditionally. Her love is strong, deep, and unmovable. She doesn't come and go like the leaves on a tree, she is the damn tree. The hurricanes, tsunamis, tornadoes, earthquakes, rain, hail, sleet, and snow in life will come but faithful and strong she will still be there in the midst of all tribulations. She loves to treat a man that's always treating her. Whether that means having a good meal ready when he gets home from work or waiting naked for him to walk in and help him relax all that stress! She represents herself and family at all times, keeps looking good, and supporting her man through all challenges.

Men always think about the sex first, never really considering what they will need in the future. See when you choose a female they're only good for one thing, a woman is good for everything. When the kids are acting crazy, you start going bald, you lose your job, your balls drop, you have prostate cancer, heart attacks, strokes, go bankrupt, parents pass away, you want to go back to school middle age, and you start going through manopause acting like you need a tampon, that woman is there. Yea I said it, MANOPAUSE!

If you're with a woman she is not waiting on you to choke and die to get your money because she served her purpose. HINT! A female has screwed you until you couldn't screw no more and now she's screwing the man she's really in love with while waiting on your life insurance to come through. That's a female for your ass!

One woman will be there by your side at all times. She will take great care of you, keeping you healthy and looking damn good no matter what your age. If you happen to pass before she does she's going to take care of the kids, fulfill your wishes, and love you for the rest of her life. That is a woman. Now you know so take a look at what you have!

MENtally Challenged

Men, take some time to examine the female choices you have made in your lifetime. Why you married who you did? Why you left who you left? Why you won't use condoms and what it cost you? Take a moment to reminisce on the woman or women you should have been with today if you knew then, what you know now.

Now look at yourself. Have you recovered from any damage or regret from past relationships? You know fellas, there's nothing wrong with going through a little therapy to help you learn some things about who you are, just saying. Or even having communication with God and asking him to show you the things you can't see and hear the things you can't hear if you feel temptation is blinding you. You know it is! Sexual healing can't solve all of your problems.

I find most men marry and reproduce with what you want for you and not what God wants for you. It's not that God did not give you what he had for you, he's probably given you more than one opportunity but you couldn't see pass the little head on your body and you let it choose for you.

For example, every now and then you run up on a good man. Sometimes he's married to the worst female ever, but has not taken the time and used resources to figure out why he's in love with that female that uses and abuses him. They just hang in there and let the marriage run its course, especially when they have kids. That's what happens when you're misguided by the little head! There is nothing feminine or weak about you taking a look at your inner-self, who you are, where you came from, and shifting your perspective a little to understand yourself. Then you will know how to stop making the same mistakes. Step outside the box and take a look at your life. We all are products of our environment so look at how you can make those better. I bet if you were looking at someone else in your shoes you'd say he must be out of his damn mind. That's right, you got some issues. Now I'm not saying you have to go all psych or anything, just take some time to reflect.

Why do you choose females over women? Are you intimidated, threatened, scared, controlling, egotistical, or even jealous of women? When you look at an attractive beautiful woman, seems like you all think about is how she's not open for business instead of long term life partner. Drop the sex act! You should not stop talking to women because they won't screw you in a week. That's a good thing dummy, that means any and everything isn't going in and out of her. She cares about herself and who she decides to share her body with.

Screwing some female a week after you met her only means your ass is dirty too!

And another thing, I can't stand for men to say a woman is high maintenance. Let me tell you something, if you see a woman who looks high maintenance and she is single that means she can afford to look the way she looks and she does not need you to maintain her appearance. She's not going to ask you and don't need you to pay for her mani and pedi, hair dresser, weave, clothes, shoes, or anything else. Now if you have a problem with that, you should wonder why you want a woman to need that from you.

What satisfaction do you get from females needing you financially the reason you leave the women who don't? It should be your offer not an obligation, that's if your desire is to treat her. It's ironic how you will meet a female that needs a make-over, turn her into high maintenance, and then complain that she's always got you spending. It's the intent of owning someone, you feel as though you made her and she wouldn't be who she is without you. Funny thing is once that upgrade goes to her head she'll want you to put out more than ever before and when you can't, she's on to the next! But you wouldn't approach the one that was doing it for herself. What kind of sense does that make?

I understand men want to feel desired and appreciated, but understand this does not have to be financially. A woman does desire you, physically and emotionally, but when it comes to financially, be happy to be a team. If it makes you feel less of a man that a woman makes more money than you, look at why you have a problem with that. Now, I agree if she is throwing it in your face and your relationship is a power struggle based on money that is a problem. Big problem!

Are you jealous if a woman is able to do things financially that you cannot afford to do for her or even for yourself? If you meet a woman who is interested in you but you back off once you find out she's a company director with her own everything and money does not impress her, there is something wrong with you! The way you impress a woman is through consideration, thoughtfulness, and most of all common sense. She doesn't have to tell you or teach you every little thing to do because you have already taken care of business even when it means taking the initiative to teach yourself.

Now don't give me the excuse of females have better sex, most smart women don't do oral or they don't have a sex drive. That's bullshit! If a woman really loves you, and you are the man she needs you to be she will be the woman you need her to be. Your sex won't just be sex. It will be a passionate connection of love making. Not five minutes of one riding the other and then you get up and leave, I said love making. That means tension, sweat, and intensity. She's going to want it all the time. And regardless of how old you get, it'll always go up for her! Didn't you read The Amazing 90!

All I see is men dating these females who clean them out. They play the game with you for a while, have your baby and drop that child support. Later on in life you find that the child is not even yours but that bitch aint offering no REFUND! She just used you to pay her rent for up-teen amount of years and didn't even offer an apology. All they say is, "Well, I thought the baby was yours." Some of them are in denial and keep lying about it even after there's proof because they don't want to acknowledge their ho ass ways!

And what's up with men actually committing to females who are constantly cheating on them. These females do not love you and have NEVER loved you. For some reason, you all ignore the signs that she doesn't want you! But you will run from the woman who was genuinely crazy about you. If your woman, wife, or significant other if you will, wants your sex to be over quickly or does not want it at all that's because she's sleeping with somebody else! She doesn't like sleeping with you because she loves sleeping with him. It disgust her to have intercourse with you so she wants to get her obligation in the relationship over with as soon as possible until she's ready to leave. That means after she stashes some of your money, gets a few cash advances off your credit cards, and gets the man she's with who's probably married his damn self, to leave his wife! See, you get sex but women get everything. And you thought you were running this game! DUMB ASS! You aint running shit!

If you are in the position right now dating a woman and you know she's a woman. You are starting to punk out and considering ending the relationship. STOP! Give yourself the opportunity of staying in a forever relationship and becoming a better man. That's one thing a man and woman do when they are in love, they become better people together. If she's not asking you for money, she works, loves you, and is committed, KEEP HER! You may never get that chance again. And don't be no sorry ass and think she needs to be patient for your love. Don't ever tell a woman she's impatient when it comes to reciprocating love in a relationship. Men are impatient. They want to fuck you in the first week, that's impatient. If you tell a man he's on a 30, 60, or 90 day rule they just keep hitting a side piece until they hit you and then on to the next game. A woman who loves you and only wants love in return has to wait for it. Oh, that's some bull! You didn't make a female wait when she asked you for some money………….oh you got that right then and there no problems. But they have to wait for your love? Please let me know, where the hell is the logic in that?

If you have already left this woman, let me tell you what to do. Stop being a punk! Get yourself together, collect your thoughts, humble yourself, and prepare to deliver an apology. They're not bad guys, it's only two words……I'm sorry. Find that woman, and step to her straight up like the man you know you can be. Do not go to her expecting her to forgive you, drop what she's doing even if she's dating someone else at this point, and pick up where you all left off acting like nothing ever happened.

Say you are sorry, you made a mistake in letting her go, you did not realize what you had or even that you were not ready for what you had. But that you are ready NOW! And if given the opportunity your main priority is to give her the amazing love in return that she had given you. You will be the man she wants and needs because she is all you want and need.

Be prepared for the blessings and happiness to follow. If she is a woman who has not already moved on and has it in her heart to forgive you because she still loves you, your life will change from that point on. If you do not rectify your mistake, you will not only live with that for the rest of your life as the punk ass you are but you may never get a chance like that again. Don't wait another day, minute, or second. Life is too short to create your own bad karma that's going to kick your ass later. Remember, life is a bitch and then you die!

Stop thinking about the other two billion females in the world that don't want your ass and will never love you the way she did. You messed up, you wrong, step to the plate and move on. With females you spend enough money you ought to have a routing and account number attached to your social! Do yourself a favor and don't spend the rest of your life as a human bank account. A woman is worth far more than your commitment, but she is worth your sacrifice. Females flip on you every day and all the time but a good woman will always and forever be; a good woman.

Always Looking for Less When You Have the Best

Men always do this! A wonderful woman will come across their path, relationship will be just fine, and they choose to complicate it. The right woman came at a time that was inconvenient for them and they chose the wrong one at their convenient time instead. God does not work on your time, matter of fact, you don't have any time. It's all his! Seeming to have a pattern of choosing the major issues over the minor, exchanges instead of relationships continue in the world today.

Most men have met the right woman at least twice, maybe even three times in their life but have always looked over them. Usually with issues that don't even make sense or are too far in advance for the stage of their relationship. They hesitate and eventually sever relationships with women but give everything beginning with material first to a female. Guess what, if you are giving your money that means she is taking your money. Do you get it, TAKING your money? Don't be a dumb ass and call her a gold digger after the "exchange" goes to hell in a handbag. She was one when you met her, so who's the dummy?!

A man who has been in long term relationships or marriages with females think they know love. But when they get blessed with the real thing, they don't know what to do with what they've never had before. If they have had love before and lost it, the next time they run up on that blessing they'll do everything they can to keep it. Never realizing, love only comes from women, lust = LOST which is exactly where that female is going to leave you. Right along with Chicago!

You cannot make a female love you, it is not in her, and she has no idea what it is either. In this time of dating, love is the word used to represent an exchange, most of the time sex for money. A way of hiding prostitution in plain sight if you will. Deals and agreements with back door angles or ill intentions are all leading to unsuccessful love and children with lower standards. Now please don't get mad at these females, it's not really their fault. Most of them started out right but because of child hood experiences, domestic violence, rape, and all that other shit caused by punk ass men they've made choices to cope with their damage. Quite frankly, I understand but I just can't do what they do.

It is absolutely hilarious to me when I see men make this mistake every time they attempt to commit and settle down. They left the right woman for a female, something that wants their money, stability, and attention, by any means necessary. That means through their favorite playgrounds like child support when they couldn't squeeze the man into marriage to get spousal too, or divorce because the man thought he could make a ho into a housewife, or even tricking through the purchase of homes, cars, designer clothes, and paying bills. Their play ground is sex, which is why they are so successful at destroying decent men because a man thinks sexually before everything else.

There are still good men in the world, they just make the same silly decisions. It's cute how their minds are motivated not to make the same mistake with females. They'll start wearing condoms like they should've been in the first damn place, have a vasectomy, and even remarry with a female they met in church instead of in the club as if that's where all the good ones are. I mean really I've got to give it to them, they try, they're just not bright enough to look deeper at themselves and the reasons why they've chosen the females they have.

Some men have the right purpose but have a completely jacked up process. Heart first, then money!

The only benefit a good man has from committing to a female is because they're not on his level. Men almost feel in control, a sense of power and comfort believing that she's never going to leave because he takes care of her. Little do they realize when you go low they bring you down to their level and almost come out with the better end of the stick when the relationship ends.

Females get the house, cars, stocks, bonds, accounts, 401ks, vacation homes, almost everything they've never worked for. Did you hear me? They've NEVER WORKED FOR IT! A female lying on her backs is the laziest job there is and in some cases makes far more money than a woman that doesn't. All of this gain by leading a man to think he had control and she loved him. They do what men ask sexually and never part their lips until a man says no to something or well of course the money dries up. Then it's all bad from there. When you're screwing a female, you're not screwing her, you're screwing yourself! Men always think they're running game but look who's really getting played? Females play the game because they are not woman enough to obtain their desires independently. They think what's between their thighs is a meal ticket which most of the time it gets them just where they were trying to go. Only problem is, it's not that far from where they started.

Unfortunately, a man's nature is sexually driven so regardless of what their minds think, they don't know how to let their brain and heart lead them in the right direction. In this books instance, Chicago had a beautiful woman, damn good woman. She wasn't much of a people person, very reserved, and confidence usually taken as arrogance. But honey, she wasn't down for nobody but her love.

She talked until she was blue in the face but he heard none of it. One thing about men, they don't hear shit! They are so used to females yapping it's like whatever to them. Only thing they understand is action, now they'll understand that in a minute. Every day he had a new excuse and claimed he had this decision as he calls it. Every man should know this about life, when you meet a good woman and that good woman loves you, there's no decision to be made!

At this point, Desire now understood that what she wanted was as rare as she is. She has a very committed and loyal love. Whatever it takes, whatever you want, be all you need kind of love. Bottom line, dude fucked up royally. He messed over the total package for a female! She was fully loaded and he got the base model with options. Well men, when you do that you must pay for each and every one of those options. Good Luck! The total package has everything you want right now and all of what you'll look for when you need it. When you take that base model with options, you'll do more than just pay for it. But you'll miss out on everything you will need later. Most people have never had real love, ever. Makes you wonder, have you really had love in your lifetime? When you look back on that one you thought loved you, did they really love you? If they had an affair, NO! If they screwed you over, NO! If they gave up on your relationship, NO! I'll tell you what love is.

What It Is & What It Aint!

Since I'm talking about all this love, we must ask ourselves what is love? Define love. Above all else, love is a blessing. Men always make the mistake of believing all women can and will love them if they entertain them. That is one of the biggest misconceptions in a man's mind. It's almost their way of convincing themselves and women that they have endless options. Let me tell you something, THEY DON'T! There is only one woman that will love you, let alone love you the best. Chicago was crazy to think any woman would ever love him the way Desire had. He'll never find that again but karma is a bitch and he's damn sure going to wish he had it.

Obviously, nobody knows what love is and what it's not. Love is a gift, even a privilege. It's a companionship and collaboration of efforts, the sharing of emotions. This begins with a connection of the hearts and minds that then makes you desire someone physically. They are stimulating you mentally and filling you up with that wonderful thing we call happiness. Love is committed and strong. It is encouraging and supportive. It is communication and consideration for a partner and the respect of a relationship.

Love is not abusive, whether that is mentally, verbally, or physically. I don't care what nobody say's, you cannot love someone and cheat on them. When you're really in love, only one person can turn you on and you won't settle for less. It doesn't even feel good for someone else to touch you or kiss you, regardless of how horny you are, you just can't do it. Love has limits and sharing your body with other people is one of them! Love is not infidelity, dishonest, unappreciative, controlling, disrespectful, irresponsible, complaining, or drama. It's not putting family before your partner. Females do not love you they love what you are doing for them. And when you can no longer do it or they meet someone who can do it better they will leave you. Think of it this way, it's a hole you will never dig yourself out of. A loan with an unbelievable interest rate intended and designed for you to never pay it off. Kind of like a cash advance.

What men fail to see is when you start off spending money on a female that means you want a gold digger. You shouldn't have to empty your pockets to receive love or is it that you really don't want love, you want the exchange. A woman's love does not cost you anything; a female acting like they love you will cost you everything. Also, no family interference. Your mother, father, sisters, and brothers all have a place so put them in it. If you don't know how to then go sleep with them but you can't have it both ways. So mama's boys, that means stop sucking your mama's tits! If you don't know how to separate your wife from your mother because you think you got it all in moms, then don't waist nobody's time. Keep shopping in the female department. If you have any of these traits in your current relationship, I suggest you evaluate what's keeping you there and what those actions may lead to in the future. Now that you know what it is, I bet you've never had it. So what are you going to do about it?

Are You Serious

Men, if you don't receive anything else out of this book. Please, please, let this stick with you......Condoms are $5. Five damn dollars. I don't know how many other ways I can say it. I mean seriously, should I start translating this into other languages you don't even speak! Child support is forever! Eighteen years of check garnishment, direct deposit, court dates, custody battles, visitation rights, mediation meetings, attorney's fees, court fees, defamation of character, slander, baby mama drama, social media humiliation, maybe even some property damage, domestic violence, and assaults charges.

This is two hundred and sixteen months, six thousand five hundred and seventy days of your life. If you didn't catch that is 216 months which equals 6,570 days. That's a sentence without a jail cell. The drama may even begin from the date of conception, which means an additional 270 days. All because going raw feels good. I understand when you are in the heat of the moment your only thought is what's dry and what's wet. I hear so many men, stupid men, saying it just doesn't feel the same. Well, let me ask you this, what feels better? Eighteen years of drama plus STD and HIV risk or five little ass dollars well spent!

Some of this shit is just getting ridiculous. Now some of you are definitely not husband material but at least be smart enough not to wife a female you know is not marriage material either. These days females are on national television telling the world who they are, what they do, and what they're about but you wife that! Funny how marriage has become a status of being the number one bitch and not the only woman in a man's life.

I find it so interesting that these men are complaining about the females they married after reality hits their ass. She took this, she did that, AND! Men have this horrible line they love to use on women these days, trying to make us accept, conform, and deal with your ho ass ways. You know what I say to that, YOU KNOW WHAT IT IS! That's right, you knew you were buying that female, she had a price tag, she gave you all the signs to let you know what she was in your life for and you wanted that. Every time you slept with her you singed on the bottom line of agreement. Hell, you didn't just sign you put your DNA on the bottom line. You thought you'd always be the big man on top and she'd always be beneath you trying to get what's in your pocket. Men love to say serve your purpose, but dumb ass you got one too when you play that game. Take some ownership in your sorry ass decision to marry and procreate with what was beneath your level and not on your level! The tragedy happens to your stupid asses and then you want stop and think about the one or two good women you had that you should've married.

Sometimes, you're even bold enough to look that woman up and think she's just supposed to take you back no questions asked. The female broke you down. This bitch made sure she never had to work another day in her life. Hint boys, if a female is asking for marriage but you're saying no and she gets pregnant, is pregnant right after a proposal, or right after you get married, it's not always just because she loves you. Know this; children are security, financial security at that! She screwed you and didn't even use grease! But notice that you always go to a woman to build back you up, but once you get up you never keep your foundation.

That woman was your foundation, so of course you are going to fall on your ass. You get money and females start calling you like a bill collectors. Then you think you need to upgrade and get caught cheating because you were trying to be a pimp! HA! Look player, stop giving 2nd what you haven't gave the 1st and you wouldn't have that problem. If you're going to be a pimp at least keep your pimping in order and your side pieces in check! You never give a ho hope, that's the combination that gets you all messed up. The ho was giving you what you wanted with no strings attached, you messed up as soon as you acted like you had some feelings as though that was your way of keeping her legs open. BIG MISTAKE! That's why they start stepping to your wife and letting their presence be known. It's to make your wife leave you because a female knows women don't tolerate that shit and once she's gone, the bimbo will have you all to herself! I told you, we are smarter than you. And the cycle continues, looking for less when you had the best. But you want a woman to be there after you hit rock bottom. No place to stay, no money, no job, or excuse me. No contract, no endorsements, no business ventures, even your entourage left your ass too. What on God's green earth makes you think we want your dumb pathetic over used ass when you come to us with nothing to bring to the table. Then you say, "I love you and have always loved you" or that "All I have to give is my heart, I wasn't ready to be the man you wanted me to be" kind of shit. Well, light bright, that's all the woman wanted in the first damn place! But noooo not now!

You've gone out and slept with more females than the NBA has games. Your shits been in more holes than a gas pump but we're supposed to accept that! Child supports coming out your checks, you owe back child support, back taxes, haven't been to the doctor, might have HIV, and you think a woman is supposed to stop her life and be all the things you need in order to get you back to where you were. Back to the top, because that's where a woman takes you. Females, take you the bottom.

If that not a leach what is?! You want to latch on and drain her dry financially, emotionally, mentally, and physically because you know you want some ass too. All the miles you've got on your stick and you want to defile her good shit! Are you serious??!! And when it's all said and done, you'll walk away, back to the egotistical dumb asshole you were in the beginning still screwing females, and on your way to the failure and self-destruction you set yourself up for. You better take your ass back to that trick and get trapped, oh excuse me, back to your "options"!

Divorce Damage

Men, this is strictly for you. I almost feel sorry for some of you who really thought who you married was "the one". People meet you and know you're hurt but nobody has really looked at the impact divorce makes on a man. Too busy talking about how much the female got in the end. Now this isn't for the women who held a man down for years, it's for you idiots who left the women and wife up the tramps. The marriage will be as long as twenty years and short as 30 days before the female you married begins her master plot and plan to destroy you, break you down, and leave with everything you have worked so hard to accomplish.

Here you are, in your 30s even 40s, married to a female you thought loved you. How cute! She flips out because you want her to stop spending, or you want to stop working so hard, or you want to change your life and stay off the street, or you're not as exciting as you used to be. She's sleeping with some punk on the side, being the ho she was all along, blah blah blah we all know the game but I don't see men changing it.

See when you met her you were spending money, and she wasn't. I'll teach you what women do in a later chapter. You're taking care of her and she's screwing your brains out. Acting like she's a good mother to your kids or getting knocked up on purpose after your proposal or honeymoon but really, when it all goes down she'll change your pockets so much the kids can't even maintain the lifestyle they've become accustomed too because daddy was so STUPID!

One day you wake up, get served, and you have to do what? START OVER! Now you're middle age, credit may be too messed up after divorce to purchase a home so, you have to rent instead. The privileges of home ownership in the future may be crushed. And if you can get a mortgage, it's pathetic you just lost and maybe even got kicked out of the home you were ten or fifteen years into paying off on a 30 year mortgage.

Meaning, you won't even OWN a home by the time you retire. See most of you didn't even catch what I just said because you're not on that level. Probably still living g-fab, the car you drive cost more than the house you live in as if you can sleep in it. You will still be paying a mortgage when you're sixty to seventy years old because you tried to make a ho into a housewife.

You skipped the good women to marry the nasty little thing that came along when you were ready to do something and she took everything. She completely destroyed you. Now I know most women want to say a mother is a job, not in this economy it's not and damn sure not if you're black! But that's just my fapinion, factual opinion.

And God forbid you are divorcing your child's step mother. That's really sorry, your children will not benefit from nothing because daddy just lost it to a female not even in relation to them. What I mean is, at least if the mother of your child dies, what's left will pass on to your kids. And when I say what's left I mean just that, minimal, see money and a fool soon part.

This is all in addition to the destruction of your pride, optimism, happiness, stability, and then some. Plus, eventually you will begin to date which is no fun either. You're older now, not as handsome as you used to be, and are having to admit yourself you kind of question who wants you? Which is honest, your metabolism has dropped, might be looking a little round in the middle, going bald, and that car doesn't start like it used to if you know what I mean. Matter of fact it's really running flat, not much you can do with that.

Most divorced men fill the empty space with their kids, almost treating them like a spouse. They feel their child is such a good kid, great kid, wonderful kid; they give them everything they want. And for the time, they may be good kids but soon disappointment will arrive. The higher you have put that child up on a pedestal, the more it will hurt you when they fall. And they will fall. Stop taking fatherhood to the extreme and letting kids make decisions on what house they want you to move to, neighborhood to live in, car to drive, it's too much control and influence.

You're almost treating them the way you did the female, giving them everything they want. Then when you do meet someone special that child will not be very happy they're around because things may change. And they may even say and do some things to get rid of them so keep the kids in their place. Your child can never be your companion so do not attempt to turn them into one.

Now as for those of you who say you are divorced because you just weren't happy. If your ex-wife started that shit, tell that ungrateful ass female thank you. It just cracks me up to hear, "We just weren't happy." You are both in good health, kids in good health, good jobs, nice home, bills getting paid on time, food in the pantry, and you're still two attractive people but this female is complaining. You do not need an unappreciative ass female anyway. She just wants out to screw other people or the person she been messing around with during the marriage, cancel that ho! And the same to men, the grass is never greener on the other side and you will pay for that mistake. We weren't happy means it was no longer a game, they're used to playing one so they leave you in order to do so.

Better or Bitter

There are so many men who believe most women are mad and bitter. Don't get it twisted, they are better! Maybe a little jaded like myself, but better. On the account of some idiot's actions, yes they want to take a break from lies, infidelity, and punk ass men! Unfortunately, these are women that have been wearing an ugly face better than they wear a pretty one for years. This is from horrible male decisions, blind ass men, and the disposable society we live in. They are tired of males who want a woman to put them on, make them somebody, and then get somebody else. And even more tired of men that are on their level but choose to date females. The females always get a ring but the women do not.

This is an inner battle of maintaining and patiently waiting for the love of a man who recognizes who they are and what they have to bring to the table. That kind of man is a dying breed and damn near extinct. Me personally, it doesn't even exist in my generation. The popularity of the fake and superficial has abolished the real love women and men should have for one another.

The women continue to attempt at love and relationships but after repetitive failures, life is pushing them to disbelief that there's a man for them. The acceptance of being alone for the rest of their lives has become more likely than ever having a companion. I find it quite ironic that when these women go out to different clubs, lounges, or bars men claim they are bitter. Sometimes they say rude, mad, or evil never taking into consideration the woman is looking at you like it's one of you idiots that made me this way. We are tired of you trying to make us your fuckable mommy! You want us to cook, clean, have babies, take care of your ass, take care of business, and fuck you. That's a FUCKABLE MOMMY!!!!! No woman is going to be that for you but a female will certainly act like it if the price is right!

You want us to treat you like a man, let you lead and we follow. All you've been doing is leading your ass straight to ditches and dirt but you expect a woman to follow you. You don't know who you are, who you want to be, you're a different man with every woman you meet but we're supposed to trust you to lead and you can't even lead your damn self! I think not. Now if a man understood that there's a substantial reason she is the way she is, and he is a good man, he would still take the time to entertain her knowing that a good man is really all she needs. He knows the potential and return of the investment if he were to obtain her love. Not worried about the smile that's not on her face but he's more concerned about the one he's going to put on it.

Now I agree there is some ownership by women in their attitude. But when is enough too much. When do we stop getting up to get knocked down? At some point you just need to walk away. I ask myself why keep trying if life is teaching you differently? Men have shown me they want poles instead of potential, peace, and prosperity. Shown me they'd rather have sex instead of success, a female on a dick not a woman behind a desk, but when she's got the picture you call her bitter. Don't get mad because she knows what it is! When you see a successful man you always see a supportive woman. She's at every ball game, event, gala, business opening, and award show dolled up and decked out supporting her man. She's compromising and sacrificing her life to help him reach his goals. But a man will not do the same for a woman in that role. You don't see no man standing behind a woman supporting her success. He's at all of her business nominations, recognition awards, promotion celebrations, holding her down and having her back like she would him. That's like me saying a man will stand behind me at all my book signings, get books out of my trunk for me, sell my books to buyers when I'm not around, and help me grow my other companies. I'm going to find a man who is willing and wants to grow an empire together, sure I will once I sprout wings and fly!

So basically you mean to tell me as a woman I'm supposed to compromise and help you meet your accomplishments but I can't meet my own using my own talents and gifts. You want me to be all into you, wrapped up in you, and in my feelings about you but you're not that way for me. All I can do is reap the benefits of what you earn from your success, which you wouldn't have without my support because there's nothing in this world you can do alone. And when you decide that you no longer want what's been there all your life, you want one of these new breed bitches you think you can just pay me off like you bought me when you were broke and we're even now that you have a little change. I met you when you didn't have shit but lint in your pocket and you think you can divide dollars by a number of years. Some of you do not like what I just said because you feel different but fuck what you feel; I'm talking what's fact! And that fact lets me know men are the most insecure and selfish creatures I have to encounter on a daily basis. I believe in making the best out of the cards you are dealt. Put your good foot down and make your soul a winner. Remember, regardless of what we try to do, every partner that comes in and out of your life changes you in some way, shape, form, or fashion.

If I took the time to ask a man if they have treated all the females across their lifetime the right way, they would all say no. So men, before you decide not to approach that woman sitting across the room, looking absolutely gorgeous but doesn't have a smile, consider that you have probably done what was done to her by someone else. Admit that you are not stepping to her because you have bad intentions and her guard is not going to let you fuck her up like the last one. She's not going to look the other way while you're cheating on her, allow you to live off of her, babysit you, let you play video games all day because you don't have a job, or be some sorry as dick on demand 24 hour rental when B.O.B is a one-time fee and last forever!

And you wonder why we throw you in the same boat together. Well, do different and you'll get treated different. Until then, you're not proving women wrong you're just proving them right. And to the men who stand around and look at a woman decked out and won't say anything but speak to that same woman when she's not looking her best, I got something for you. When you walk by the best and speak to the half-dressed there are several things to be said about you. You're lazy, insecure, and weak so don't act like that woman is stuck up because you aint shit!

Women do not to want to hate you, we want to love you. Believe it or not, I love you and that's the reason why I'm writing this. I can't stand seeing men look so pathetic. Step to that woman correctly, and you may be surprised it could be the best woman you've ever met in your life. Most of the time a woman with the most severe relationship damage is usually a hell of a woman. They have the most amazing love. Know this before you approach them and be ready. Don't be no punk! By the way, don't try something just to try it. Learn from Chicago, don't start nothing you can't finish!

Can You Afford It?

When we think being ready for love we usually think that means, career, money, cars and a home. The term "set" comes to mind. Actually, the first thing you should think about is are you equipped mentally, emotionally, and physically for the toll dating can take on you. Love has consequences too, can you afford them? The most valuable and necessary preparation is emotional improvement. Now listen we've all incurred issues through failed relationships leaving us with negative perspectives, hesitating hearts, and other emotional baggage. So when we decide to pick ourselves up and try again we need to be more prepared this time than we were the last.

First we need to determine if we are damaged goods. Forget if you have a chance with love, does love have a chance with you? Are we shutting good things down before they even start? Are we subconsciously sabotaging great relationships because we have not corrected the damage that was done to us by another or even by ourselves?

We need to be prepared for the worst, another round of disappointment of course, but we also have to hope for the best. If you find love or love finds you the next time you meet someone special can you appreciate the real thing? Are you able to be happy if you've never been? Will you know love if you've never had it?

For women, emotional hesitation is normal but we are always ready to love, waiting to love, and wanting to love. Men however, are truly emotionally scared. I believe they see the hurt we struggle with after a disappointing relationship and how long it takes to recover from it. In all honesty, a man would rather give you his money before he ever gives you his heart. That's why females have two, three, four, five men, but a woman can't find one to save her life.

See money is easier, it's what they know. Trained to think, get the money and women will follow but it's actually females who follow. Actually females who flock! A woman doesn't need or want them financially; their desire is emotional and mental. The only financial thinking they have with men is to start moving mountains and making dreams come true through supporting each other.

Men can't afford women because it's too hard. They have no idea how to do it, but it's simple. The same way you took care of that trash, give that to a woman. You will be absolutely amazed out of your mind what you will receive in return. Women want men to display the intangible things of life, but men are visual creatures so it's very hard. Give love to what is down to ride, not what is always riding you!

So You THINK You Want A Woman?

Alright, so you've almost finished the book and have decided to make a change. This is so simple but just like females men always complicated things that have no complication. You are now wondering what to do and what not to do in order to find a woman. I would like to think common sense would tell you that if you knew what to do with a woman then you would know how to get one, but I forgot everybody doesn't have common sense. Most of the time people do, they just don't use it. First of all, stop the games. I know it's hard because most of you have been doing it all your life and you don't know different. At this point you have no idea how to approach a woman but always remember she is a lady first and foremost. You speak to and respect her as such. No cheesy lines necessary just be yourself. Stop acting like you're something you're not.

Make sure you have become eligible before you even get started. That means making sure you have your shit together. Now I'm not saying have a big house, fancy car, perfect credit, a college degree, and a bunch of money. I'm saying you can't live with your mother, be unemployed, no goals, no manners, no intellect, and other things of that nature. Make sure you dress nice and carry yourself in a strong confident and not cocky way.

By the way, dressing does not mean a pimp suit with alligator boots every day of the week. It just means look nice whether you're a pretty boy faded and laid, or not so pretty but clean cut. I know you would love to tell me about how hard it is to get a job if you don't have one. I understand and this is what I'm going to tell you, Jesus was a carpenter. If you can't find a job, make a job! Women make apples out of oranges every damn day. Be motivated and determined to have some level of success and satisfaction in life. A woman has no complaints if you are a good man and paying your bills with your own talents, whatever that maybe within reason. Translation, LEGALLY!

By the way, that whole "The system is keeping me down thing." Take a second and get ready for what I'm about to pass to you, go long, are you ready? Watch this, you are trying to keep your own women down by promoting poles, $20s, $50s, & $100s but you're actually keeping yourself down too. I can't stress this enough, you can't do anything to a woman without doing it to yourself. Understand this, we are one. "The system" is great at keeping your ass on corners and out of corporate. With this mentality you end up in prison or on child support, which by the way are both owned by "the system". It influenced your dumb ass by using your women and your money to keep you down and hand you directly over to "the system". And the women who are resilient to this change, meaning the women who get it off the top not the females who get it from the bottom, remain single and some even get selected by "the system". Don't get mad at "the system" because it wouldn't be one if you'd stop getting your ass in it! In order to do this you need to understand why there is a system.

 Everybody always wants to talk about they got haters. Haters hate on you because you have something they don't or can do something they can't. Ok, that means the system is the biggest hater that ever lived. If you idiots knew who you were you would know why there is a system. "The system" knows who you are, it knows you are smarter than the rest, stronger than the rest, and that you can survive what it can't that's why it's hating on you. To be quite honest, although there are a few imitations and duplications left at random, "the system" stopped being produced a long time ago. But it is you who bought it and became the new owner so you could continue to make it yourself. See your ass isn't even smart enough to catch that! It was too deep for your shallow ass, didn't have big nipples and a hole in it so you don't know what to do with it. Conspire on that silly rabbit! You're not ready boo, try again!

To all my men not balling out of control but you just do alright for yourself; please understand a man is not measured by his money nor by the amount of ass he's hit in his years of living. You know this so stop acting like your brand new! Know what it means to take a woman out for a walk in the park to get to know her; it doesn't have to be a fancy dinner! If you can hold a conversation with her then you both have better chances of sharing a connection. Don't take her out somewhere and try to cop a feel, seriously you'll get it when the time is right. When the time is right, it's definitely worth waiting for.

Try to do some things together, if you don't want to take her out for dinner then cook your best meal and invite her over. Get to know her likes, dislikes, and what she's looking for so you'll have a better understanding of where you stand. Remain honest, thoughtful, and respectful. Those three things will take you further with any woman than they ever will with a female. Women do not ask for much so learn to appreciate that. We want you more than we'll ever need you. That's a good thing so stop acting like it's not.

The Reality

I know your girl was raw! But that's how the world is today, dating today is just that, raw. We are living in this saturated society where men feel like they can drop this one and just get a new one. It's almost worse for women because they have to worry about so much when it comes to men. Not just thinking if he's the one or not, but is he a ho, broke, down low, liar, cheater, and has he been tested? We don't just have to worry about men screwing around with other women but we have to watch out for men screwing other men too!

For men this is different, they may worry about a female being faithful, does she have her stuff together, but when it comes to sleeping with other females some men are even okay with if as long as they can get in on the action. SICK! Or if she's messing around, they just mess around too and call it even. They fail to realize they have as many issues to worry about when it comes to finding a good woman as we do finding a good man. Do men realize that most beautiful and intelligent women are single? CEOs, Vice Presidents, and Directors, of companies are well educated, fine as hell, and single but every female on the street has a man. I would think they'd be chasing after them, that is, if they want a good woman, which is still in question!

Men have the assumption they can just pick one when they are ready to stick with one and that female will love them. No, a female cannot and will never be a woman. Get that through your head. This won't be apparent to a man until he stops giving her the attention she was receiving in the beginning, puts her on a budget, and ultimately this will lead to "Oh honey it didn't mean anything, you're just never around." When all is said and done, we all want love and most of the time we're too dumb to realize we are what I call just plain lost, loving lust.

Love is a drug for women and sex is a drug for men. When you love someone, you ignore all the things you shouldn't and when they're gone you have to come off that high you had of happiness. For men, sex blinds them, makes them spend money, lie, cheat, risk their life and that of others. Sex destroys their lives, their children's lives, and consecutively this kills the morals and values of the future that they're going to live long enough to see. Dumb Asses! And they have the nerve to be shaking their head at their kids and grandkids like they didn't start this shit.

Time for rehab! Heartbreak is going to put you on an emotional ride through sadness, frustration, disappointment, and anger. No radio, no television, possibly even nothing at all because it reminds you of that person you want so desperately to forget. Just like a drug you must recover before you can make a change and most likely you will never be the same. The more times we try love with no success, the less belief we have. Every experience takes a piece of you and ultimately changes your life. Some say it's better to have loved and lost than to never have loved at all. For me, I say that's bullshit!

You can't miss what you never had. Desire would love to have never met Chicago than to experience what she did. It becomes more than an emotional fight but a spiritual fight too because God is supposed to be capable of everything, even sending someone made for us. To believe in God is to have faith and believe in love. We are made to love, why is that so difficult to do? Well, women are but the jury is still out on men!

There's somebody for everybody they say but these days I don't find it to be true. I see nothing but men getting with the trash and not the class. Men never entertain the women who can match their success, intelligence, money, or business. They say that's what they want but it's not, at the end of the day they always marry females and the women remain single. Sticking to the usual routine and leaving the long term for the short term.

More beautiful accomplished black women have begun to date outside of their race, which there is nothing wrong with. But I'm sure most of them would rather be able to love their own though. Me, I have to stay true to myself, and I love my fine ass brothers! Funny thing is I'm very single! And I don't want to hear "Oh you just haven't met the right one." This may very well be true, but just in case, myself and a lot of other women need to be prepared if that's false. The quality, character, and conscience of men has depleted tremendously. Only time will tell, all we can do is keep living.

To the women, ladies please stay beautiful, intelligent, confident, independent, and strong. Don't accept nothing less than your worth and never lower your standards no matter what the trend is. Funny how men say we're supposedly so messed up and have all these issues but I've got to say, we're out here doing the damn thing. We are always building this, running that, starting this, and owning that. If we are all messed up, we wear our scars quite well don't you think! So the next time a man breaks your heart ladies, remember that you are unstoppable and he couldn't last one day in your shoes. We got this and we're still holding their sorry asses down! We are extraordinary women of today and the wisest of tomorrow. HOLLA!

I don't expect this book to be the bible for relationships, love, and life by any means. Again, this is not meant to be a man bashing book. It is only meant to be an enlightening opinion and unspoken perspective written from experience and observation. If you are taking it personal, you're probably discussed in a not so positive way. Men, now that you have read this let's just say you have went to Love's College so graduate and use that damn knowledge. You know better, so DO BETTER!

I'm sure you're wondering what happened to Porsha and Desire. Well, I left KC and moved to pursue acting in Hollywood. After my last dating experience I realized there was nothing worth staying there for so I dashed. I needed to move, the job market was terrible, my family was crazy as hell, and besides there were no men that interest me especially after the last one. I know they always say it's who you are and not where you live, the same issues can follow you. That's not always true. Finally, I obtained my dream position as a television host for some of the leading shows on several networks. I have definitely found my calling and I've waited too long to reach my full potential with all this personality I have! Why not move to money and men! If KC wasn't working for me something else will. HEEEEEEY!

As for Desire, KC is still home to her but she travels a lot for her career and in addition to her many talents, she became an author of a damn good book. Every time we talk she's lining up book signings all over the U.S. Girlfriend is smart as hell, I can't help but admire her drive. Of course we are still single but I must admit I've been looking for love. Desire on the other hand, she doesn't even say the word after Chicago. I remember her saying, "I'm sick of this. Everybody says just get over it. FUCK THAT! He must be out of his monkey ass damn mind. There will definitely be some gain for all this pain."

I couldn't blame her though; she's a very determined and ambitious person. She's really money motivated and was definitely the wrong one to be messing with. You always want her behind you, never against you. But I knew she still loved him, didn't matter how angry she was. Just think, if she went that hard on him through anger, imagine what she would've done for him through love. Only question was, when he realized he ruined a good thing, would he know what to do to get her back? Yes, I said when! Men may be the masterminds of masking their feelings but I know they feel something. And he was definitely going to miss her when she was gone. Everybody makes mistakes, granted his was a little more foolish than most. Whether she'll admit it or not, I believe if he showed up like a REAL man she would forgive him and work it out. Well, he'd be doing most of the work but it's worth it. At least I hope he does, so I'll know there's some hope for myself.

Damn, got me in my feelings again and don't act like you weren't thinking it too. I wish the love of my life would get on some act right. It's never too late to make something right, right? Besides, make up sex is the best sex, ok let me stop. In the meantime, girlfriend figured she's going to get compensated for that bullshit.....and boy did she ever. Now don't say she's crazy, females do it all the time. Men fuck them too but there's a difference, they pay on the spot!!!! If you ask me, she did him a favor and she didn't make him pay out of pocket. Desire is not the slash tires, curse you out, and key your car type. When she's mad that bitch aint bad, she's brilliant. She capitalized on receiving her compensation in-directly, I told you she's brilliant! She turned his bullshit into Benjamin's. Because that's what a woman does, we make the impossible possible 24/7. I know you all want to ask, is that going to make her feel better? Her answer will be, "You damn right! The same way busting nuts makes him feel good is the same way busting his ass is going to make me feel good!"

Whew, I'd hate to be him but she really loved him and no matter how you look at it, he was wrong. She always said, "That's what heartbreak stems from. When you don't get what you want out of a relationship, no matter how little you asked for, you are heartbroken. A man got what he wanted and kept rolling, while the woman is left empty handed. His actions set my eyes on a new desired result that I don't depend on him for. He got his, now I'm getting mine!"

Watch out Chicago; pick your face up boo. There's no winning when she starts coming for that ass. She's going to pull out all the stops for you baby, red carpet on the way! Don't hate! And don't call her immature because she didn't just let it go. That's what his dumb ass wanted her to do. Hell, that's what they all want you to do. Don't read this and say, "Damn he messed her all up.", because she told it like it was, no sugar added! Men, you want to fuck a woman like you're a grown ass man, so deal with your truth like a grown ass man.

All she did was say what most women are thinking only she just delivered it like they do their bullshit, the only way they understand it, the only way they feel it, RAW. They mess a woman over and say "It is what it is.", no apologies. You're just supposed to deal with it, so here, DEAL WITH IT! That's how you like it, well here it is! If you ask me they might as well go on and do the damn thing. Get it over with because they'll never find anybody like each other. He needs to face it because he can't replace it. Grow some balls, call her, send her an email, hell better yet take his ass to KC and clean up the mess he made. I believe that he cared something deep for her to do what he did in the beginning and even through the months after, he just didn't deal with it like a man. She didn't hate him; she was pissed at him for running like a little punk and not being a man about it. In my opinion, man today means boy over 21 and grown man means old ass boy! I bet that fool wish he said something to her ass now.

She says "The only special woman in a man's life is the one on his dick right now. That's why I tell all these punks I'm not interested. Not interested in you acting like you want me, acting like I'm the only one, then acting like you love me, and leaving my ass with a sorry excuse. If you want to act then take your ass to Hollywood! There are no awards to be given here. The standing ovation went to Chicago! There's plenty of dick in the stores so I don't need yours! Money never disappoints Porsha, men always do."

I know that's right! She keeps on keeping on, working on a new book and business coming soon. Still hasn't dated since then so I kind of believe her when she says "Sure I'll date, when Jesus returns! Right now all these men look alike, don't shit change but the size of their dicks!" She cracks me up, and I know it sounds crazy but she's not kidding. At one point in time all she wanted was Chicago and now I don't think she has it in her to give anyone else the time of day.

She says, "Why deal with men when you can have Ben Franklin and the B.O.B. you've always dreamed of. It can spin, vibrate, pulsate, and do all the things his dick can't do. Men got this twisted, we can manufacture their parts but you can't manufacture this! I'm glad God made man first, because by the time he made woman he'd had a little practice!" Practice makes perfect! I told you she lays it on out there. Girlfriend has become a best-selling author; I never would've thought she had it in her to write like that. I love how people always mistake her youth for lack of wisdom but they are a long ways from the truth, she was just fooled for the last time. I'm proud of her and I know she's proud of me too. Now if anything changes in the men, love, and relationships department I'll be sure to let you know. Until then……men, change the game………….

Women, you're next!

That was quick right, this is not a story, it's real. And just
like life...it's short!

www.ingramcontent.com/pod-product-compliance
Lightning Source LLC
Chambersburg PA
CBHW060433090426
42733CB00011B/2252